MIKE HOGAN

Warren Publishing, Inc.

Published by Warren Publishing, Inc.
www.warrenpublishing.net

ISBN: 978-1-886057-88-3

Library of Congress Catalog Number:
2009939776

Printed in the United States of America

DEDICATION

This book is dedicated to my wonderful wife, Gayle,
whose tireless support of both me and my first attempt at writing made
this collection of pirate tales a reality.

ACKNOWLEDGEMENTS

In addition to my wife, I have been unbelievably lucky to have had Cathy Brophy, President of Warren Publishing, Inc., as my publisher. It is just impossible not to succeed if you are working with her — she just won't let you fail! Furthermore, her extremely intelligent daughter, Dr. Tasha Warren has been my relentless editor. She is so accomplished that within three short weeks she was able to insert herself into my brain and determine what I really wanted to say in the first place. She even understands my somewhat unusual sense of humor and has added more than one very wry comment to the text. I also need to thank or blame our close friends and neighbors, Judy and Terry Beers, publishers of *Southcoast* magazine, for getting me to start writing in the first place. Needless to say, there is my very good and patient comrade, Bill Quattlebaum, a true computer guru, who has put up with my daily struggles to deal with a technology that is totally beyond me, since I was born at least one hundred years later than I should have been. Finally, I have to thank my favorite author and my continuing source of inspiration, Terrance Zepke.

iv

AUTHOR'S FOREWORD

So, what do I know about pirates anyway?   The correct answer would have been not very much for the first forty-one years that I lived in North Carolina. My wife and I were transplanted Midwesterners who emigrated to the state in 1960, never even having seen the ocean. We settled in the distinctly academic atmosphere of Chapel Hill, where I attended graduate school. A few years and degrees later, I joined the National Institutes of Health. There I was absorbed in data analysis, biostatistical research, the politics of science, administrative policy, and program development -- as well as some graduate school teaching on the side. Given that type of background, you may ask, what would inspire me to write a book on pirates?

When we retired early to the Cape Fear region of coastal North Carolina, we were immediately thrust into a whole new environment. Among other things, I suddenly became aware of the real world of pirates. Or, perhaps I should say the world of real pirates. The discovery that Stede Bonnet, possibly the most inept buccaneer to ever sail the seas, was accidentally apprehended just four blocks from our new house prior to being transported to Charleston and hanged peaked my curiosity even further. What had begun as a casual interest quickly blossomed into something much more intense.

Finally, as you may have gathered from my name, I am Irish to the core. Therefore, I cannot resist listening to and, especially, telling good stories. While the pirates of the Golden Age (1690-1730) and their predecessors were almost always of questionable character at best, their stories are certainly entertaining. In fact, if I were a writer of fiction creating these stories from whole cloth, you might find some of them to be a bit too hard to believe.

PIRATES!...PIRATES!...PIRATES! has a number of special features that distinguish it from other books on buccaneers. Much, if not most of what we really know about the pirates of the Golden Age and their predecessors is based on oral history, folklore, or myth. While this book is as historically accurate as possible, it is written from a storyteller's, rather than an historian's, perspective. As a result, if more than one credible version of a pirate's story exists, I will certainly include the more colorful one.

Of course, this book covers the most notorious male buccaneers. In addition, it highlights the petticoat pirates as well, focusing on more female pirates than are generally featured in other pirate books. There are also chapters on some of the greatest pirate chasers in history, including Julius Caesar and Thomas Jefferson, and a concluding chapter on modern-day pirates and those who pursue them.

I really hope that you will enjoy traveling back three hundred or more years in history and immersing yourselves into the lives and times of these reprehensible but fascinating individuals.

CONTENTS

Dedication…………………………………………………………..…..……i

Acknowledgements…………………………………………..……… iii

Author's Forword…………………………………………....…….…v

PART I:

Some of the Most Infamous Male Pirates of all Times

Chapter One: Eustace the "Black Monk"……………….…..…………… 5

Chapter Two: Sir Francis Drake, "El Draque" …………..…...…...… 8

Chapter Three: Sir Henry Morgan, King of Pirates………..….. 11

Chapter Four: The Evolution of the Jolly Roger…...…………..…15

A Collection of Personalized Jolly Rogers.....................…………..19

Chapter Five: Thomas Tew, the Rhode Island Pirate………………20

Chapter Six: Henry "Long Ben" Avery, the Arch Pirate……...…..…25

Chapter Seven: William Kidd, Unlucky Privateer or Ruthless Pirate?...28

Chapter Eight: John Redfield, the Unknown Pirate………..….……33

Chapter Nine: Samuel "Black Sam" Bellamy, the Prince of Pirates....36

Chapter Ten: Charles Vane, the Unluckiest Pirate of Them All……...39

Chapter Eleven: Benjamin Hornigold, the Pirate Tutor..………..……42

Chapter Twelve: Edward Teach (Blackbeard), the "Fury from Hell"….44

Chapter Thirteen: Stede Bonnet, the Gentleman Pirate…...……..…49

Chapter Fourteen: Edward "Ned" Low, Avery's Main Rival

for the "Most Despicable Pirate"..………..……...…55

Chapter Fifteen: Bartholomew "Black Bart" Roberts, the Last

Great Pirate of the Golden Age………...…………… 58

Chapter Sixteen: John "Calico Jack" Rackham, One of the Most

Over-rated Pirates…………......................…........…........62

Chapter Seventeen: Christopher Condent, a Ruthless but

Successful Pirate …………..........................…….....…64

Chapter Eighteen: Edward England, Living Proof That

No Good Deed Goes Unpunished …………………….........…66

Chapter Nineteen: William Fly, the Shortest Pirate Career…….........68

Chapter Twenty: William "Billy" Lewis, the Devil's Disciple…........70

Chapter Twenty-one: John Paul Jones, English Pirate and Father

of the American Navy………......................…........…73

Chapter Twenty-two: Jean Lafitte, Villain or American Hero?..........77

PART II:

The Petticoat Pirates

Chapter Twenty-three: Alfhild, the Viking Princess…............…… 83

Chapter Twenty-four: Lady Mary (Elizabeth) Pettigrew,

a Pirate in Disguise ……............................…........……85

Chapter Twenty-five: Grace O'Malley, Pirate Queen of Ireland …… 87

Chapter Twenty-six: Anne Bonny, the Scourge of the Carolinas…….90

Chapter Twenty-seven: Mary Read, the Other Half of the

Deadly Petticoat Duo……............................…........93

Chapter Twenty-eight: Madame Cheng, Prostitute and Incredibly

Successful Pirate Queen of the South China Sea……………95

Chapter Twenty-nine: Rachel Wall, the First American-born

Petticoat Pirate……............................…........97

Chapter Thirty: Sadie the Goat and the New York River Pirates…….99

Chapter Thirty-one: Gunpowder Gertie and the *Tyrant Queen*.......101

PART III:

The Pirate Chasers

Chapter Thirty-two: Julius Caesar, Pirate Captive and Chaser.........107

Chapter Thirty-three: Pompey the Great. Perhaps the Ultimate
Pirate Pursuer...109

Chapter Thirty-four: Woodes Rogers, the Greatest Pirate Chaser
of the Golden Age..111

Chapter Thirty-five: Thomas Jefferson and the Barbary Pirates.......114

Chapter Thirty-six: Modern Pirates and Those Who Pursue Them...116

Glossary...120

Endnotes...126

About The Author...143

PART I:

SOME OF THE MOST INFAMOUS
MALE PIRATES OF ALL TIMES

Mike Hogan

*P*erhaps it is useful to begin this collection of pirate tales, primarily from the "Golden Age" (1690-1730), with a question: Why would any man choose to be a pirate in the first place? Living conditions on a pirate vessel were usually deplorable. The work was often either excessively difficult or marked by inactivity and boredom. Potable water was scarce. Food was rarely appetizing, even when free of weevils and other uninvited dinner guests. Overcrowding, the usual unsanitary living conditions prevailing on board ship, and lack of fruit and appropriate medicines rendered scurvy and a plethora of communicable diseases the pirate's almost constant companion. Life was difficult and usually brief. The average lifespan of a pirate in the 1700's was only twenty-seven years.[1] His career often ended between one and three years after it began. Moreover, it typically ended in death from disease, being lost at sea, wounds received in battle, or at the end of a rope on a gallows! Hardly the stuff of a pirate recruitment poster.

On the other hand, if you weren't a member of nobility, the landed gentry (which was often the same thing), or the slowly emerging merchant class, then you were likely to be completely uneducated, deeply immersed in poverty with little or no hope for the future, and undoubtedly facing a very short and unpleasant lifetime.

Furthermore, as my favorite author on pirates of this era, Terrance Zepke, has noted:[2]

> What most people don't realize is that piracy wasn't so much about getting rich as it was about having a way to live life on one's own terms.

Living one's life on one's own terms is not all that common even in today's world. So it must have had a much greater attraction to those of three and four centuries ago when opportunities to do so were far more limited.

Furthermore, the unattractive living conditions and short lifespan endured by pirates applied similarly to sailors aboard merchant ships and vessels of war, with the usual exception of overcrowding and death by hanging. Pirates, however, lived under a much more democratic regime than their law-abiding counterparts. They had an equal vote in all decisions made about their ship's mission. They could even remove their captain by majority vote if they were unhappy with his leadership. Furthermore, all participated in their ship's ill-gotten gains, usually based on a share system. Finally, when sufficient booty had been acquired or supplies exhausted, they could dock in some safe harbor or port, eat and drink their fill, and enjoy the company of local women for several days or even weeks. Throw in the added element of adventure and the possibility of large rewards, and it is not difficult to see why so many chose to live the life of a pirate.

But poverty and a short, hard life had always been the fate of the majority of earth's residents, so why was the Golden Age the historical heyday of piracy? The answer can be found in examining two other concurrent events that contributed significantly to the explosive growth in the number of pirates sailing the seas during this era.

The compressed period of the Golden Age, a mere historical blink-of-the-eye, was an era of greatly expanding mercantile trade between the American continent, Europe and the Bahamas. And the marked increase in mercantile activity also meant a parallel increase in opportunities for pirates to ply their craft.

As Terrance Zepke[3] has hypothesized, one underlying reason for the rapid growth of piracy during the peak of the Golden Age was the end in 1713 of Queen Anne's War, or War of Spanish Succession, as it was known in Europe. This cessation of hostilities led to the unemployment of 35,000 sailors, privateers serving under government contracts and runaway or freed slaves. Many of these former warriors sought to earn their livings in a field for which their martial training and sea-based experiences made them particularly well qualified -- piracy.

Yet, even if we can bring ourselves to understand the attraction of piracy to those who were its practitioners, why do we continue to be so fascinated with pirates today? The individuals who chose a life of piracy upon the open seas were a far cry from the often gallant, romantic, brave, and essentially patriotic heroes of the silver screen. They were, for the most part, thieves, rapists, sadistic torturers, and even murderers. But, they were bold; and while their individual tales varied considerably from one pirate to the next, most were colorful and often fascinating.

Chapter One: Eustace the "Black Monk"

*A*lthough unfamiliar to most modern buccaneer enthusiasts, Eustace the "Black Monk" is included by Terrance Zepke in her list of the top twenty most infamous pirates.[4] Much of what we know about Eustace comes from the modern translation of a poetic biography written about him in a primitive form of French during the middle of the thirteenth century[5]. Reading this impressive work is akin to reading a modern translation of Beowulf or the Canterbury Tales, i.e., the language and style of writing is rather archaic and occasionally bawdy. Nevertheless, Eustace's story certainly seems like an appropriate beginning for this brief history of the raiders of the high seas, even though he predates the Golden Age of Piracy by many centuries. Think Richard the Lion Hearted, Robin Hood, the Magna Carta, etc., to put this era into the proper time-perspective.

Eustace was born around 1170 at Courset near Boulogne in Burgundy, which is now part of France. He was one of several sons born to Baudoin Buskes, a lord or peer of Boulogne. Buskes usually referred to himself as the chevalier de Boulenois.[6,7]

A likely apocryphal but widely believed tale of the era suggests that at a young age Eustace was sent to Toledo, Spain, where he is reputed to have studied the black arts or sorcery, at which he was said to have excelled. He is even rumored to have made a deal with the Devil, who promised him that he would live until he had performed sufficient evil in the world, and then die at sea. More realistically, he was probably sent to the Mediterranean to learn the art of seamanship.

Upon his return to Burgundy at some unknown date, he became a Benedictine monk, joining St. Vulmar's Abbey in Samer near Calais[8]. Details of his brief religious vocation are rather vague. The French, who were overwhelmingly Catholic in this era, certainly regarded the religious life as a socially acceptable occupation for a male offspring. By no means did it necessarily imply that the individual in question was particularly pious or devout. On the other hand, Eustace's presumed association with the Devil is undoubtedly a folk tale at best. So, the apparent contradiction between the two is not as pronounced as it may seem upon first reading.

In any event, Eustace is said to have left the monastery to avenge the murder of his father, which supposedly took place sometime after 1190.[9] He pled his charge against Hainfrois de Hersinghen[10] at the court of the Count of Boulogne. This was still the period when serious legal cases dependent upon circumstantial evidence were resolved through trial by combat. In this particular instance, the armed combat went against Eustace's champion, or representative, and Eustace lost both his complaint and his champion. But he did gain what was certainly not his last lifetime enemy.

By 1202 documentation exists that Eustace was now serving as seneschal to this same Count of Boulogne.[11,12] Unfortunately, Hainfrois de Hersinghen gained access to the Count's confidence and convinced him that Eustace was guilty of mismanagement of his office. When ordered to appear before the Count and offer his defense, Eustace elected to disappear from the country after declaring that this charge was nothing more than a groundless attempt to imprison him. In retaliation, the Count declared him an outlaw, seized his holdings, and burned his fields. Not one to suffer an affront lightly, Eustace is said to have burned two of the Count's mills to the ground on the day of Count Renaud's betrothal (symbolic wedding candles according to Eustad[13]) before fleeing France and offering his services to King John of England.[14]

A more colorful version of this story claims that Eustace stayed in Burgundy for a year or more after the mill-burning incident, playing an additional number of retaliatory "pranks" on the Count.[15] According to this version, once when Renaud and his men were pursuing Eustace, who had disguised himself as a White monk and attended a banquet with Renaud, they failed to apprehend him but instead captured two of his men. The Count ordered that the two accomplices be blinded as punishment for being in Eustace's service. Eustace immediately responded by seizing five of the Count's horsemen and cutting the feet off four of them. He sent the fifth back to the Count, after removing his tongue, with the severed feet and a message or note that he was trading four pairs of feet for four eyes.[16]

In any event, once Eustace reached England, King John put his services to good use. The King equipped him with up to thirty galleys, bade him to attack Normandy and the French positions in the Channel Islands, and thereby helped launch his pirate career sometime between 1205-1208.[17] Some might argue that Eustace actually launched his career as a privateer rather than as a pirate. As is noted in the Glossary, there is a fine but all-important distinction between the two professions. A pirate plundered the seas (and, occasionally the land) as he saw fit, unconstrained by allegiances to any country or monarch. By the 1600's a privateer had a written contract with a given monarch that stated that he was acting on the monarch's behalf. In turn, the contract of Letter of Marque dictated which country's ships could be attacked and guaranteed the Monarch a percentage of all booty taken. This difference could be extremely important if the privateer or pirate was apprehended and placed on trial by the enemy. Regardless of the label you apply to him, Eustace proved himself to be more than a match for the King's challenge.

After a number of successful raids on the coast of Normandy, Eustace, his brothers and his fleet moved on to the Channel Isles. The armed islanders, led by a Castilian, made the mistake of confronting Eustace and his men immediately upon their landing.[18]   A bloody melee ensued during which, according to Eustace's biographer[19] "... many a corpse was made." After his total victory, Eustace supposedly invaded the rest of the isles, leaving nothing unburned or unpillaged. King John was so pleased with all that they had accomplished, that he is said to have turned the Channel Isles over to the control of Eustace and his brothers.

On the whole, the relationship between Eustace and King John was quite congenial. John is rumored to have lent Eustace four hundred silver marks to rebuild a castle in London (valued at 1,000 silver marks), which he had already given to the pirate.[20]

As so often seemed to occur in the Black Monk's troubled life, his cordial relationship with King John was not to endure. His old nemesis, Renaud the Count of Boulogne, had a falling out with the French Prince Philip II and sought safety in England.[21] Eventually, he formed an alliance with King John. Fearing that his old foe would intervene against him, Eustace elected to flee to France in 1212 and offer his services to the French King Louis through his son Philip II. His offer was readily accepted.

Eustace sided with the rebel English barons in 1215 when they revolted against King John, and may have been involved in smuggling arms and other critical supplies to them. He was also the naval key to Louis' invasion of England.

On August 24, 1217[22] a massive sea battle was initiated between the French, led by Eustace, and the English. At first, the French clearly held the upper hand, and a large number of the enemy were slain. Recall that Eustace supposedly possessed the power to make his ship invisible as part of his pact with the Devil. Eventually, Eustace's ship was separated from the remainder of his fleet and surrounded by the English. At the beginning of this many versus one battle, the English encountered fierce resistance from the French defenders and were unable to board Eustace's vessel. However, they finally threw large cauldrons of lime into the water around the Black Monk's ship, thereby blinding the French who were downwind from the English.[23] The English boarded the lone French ship, subdued the French crew, and found Eustace supposedly hiding below deck. Upon being captured, he was promptly beheaded.[24]

The French invasion effort quickly collapsed. As a result of the ensuing treaty of Lambeth in September of 1217, Louis renounced all claims to the English throne, and obviously, Eustace's brothers were forced to abandon the Channel Islands.

Chapter Two: Sir Francis Drake, "El Draque"

*I*f you only know the name of one pirate (Spanish perspective) or heroic privateer (English perspective) prior to the onset of the Golden Age, that name is most likely to be that of Sir Francis Drake. Sir Francis, or "the Dragon" as he was called in a play of words on his last name by his Spanish detractors,[25] was clearly the best-known English seaman of the Elizabethan era. He was also the scourge of the Spanish Main, the English privateer who accumulated the most booty ever seized from the Spanish empire,[26] and the vice admiral most responsible for the defeat of the Spanish Armada. Even the name of his flagship, the *Golden Hind,*[27] rivals that of Blackbeard's *Queen Anne's Revenge* when it comes to popular recognition.

Most historians seem to feel that Drake was born around 1540 in Plymouth, England[28] to a Protestant, tenant-farming family in an area that was largely populated by Catholics. As a result, during the Prayer Book Rebellion against King Henry VIII[29], he and his family were forced to leave their home and seek refuge in Protestant Kent.

In 1556, along with his cousin, Sir John Hawkins, Drake made his maiden voyage to the Americas on a ship owned by the Hawkins family. They were engaged in smuggling various supplies to Spanish colonists. While the potential for enormous profit was great, so was the risk involved in defying Spanish law. On their final trip in 1557 or 1558,[30] luck ran out. They were trapped in the port of San Juan de Ulua, Mexico, by a Spanish naval fleet in pursuit of English smugglers. The ensuing battle was brief, intense, and distinctly one-sided. The outnumbered English were soon overcome, with only two[31] of their six vessels managing to escape. Fortunately, these two heavily damaged ships were the vessels commanded by Drake and Hawkins. This brutal battle along with a strong anti-Catholic sentiment from his youth may well have been the source of Drake's lifelong animosity toward the Spanish.

Drake now focused his career on raiding along the Spanish Main, a region of 16th and 17th century Spanish America that extended from the Isthmus of Panama to the mouth of the Orinoco River in Venezuela. In July 1572 he attacked the town of Nombre de Dios, which he had scouted six months previously disguised as a Spanish merchant. His objective was the King's treasure house, which was located in the town's harbor. His brother John and a small portion of their force created a diversion on the western side of the town, while Drake and the remainder of his force assaulted the repository on the eastern side. Drake's men broke down the heavy doors to the treasure house only to discover that it was either empty or contained nothing but a small pile of silver bars. Apparently, a fleet of treasure ships had recently sailed from Nombre de Dios to Spain with the rest of its accumulated wealth. Drake was shot in the thigh during the conflict and eventually passed out from loss of blood. His men became panicked without Drake in command and quickly returned to their camp with their wounded captain but no booty.[32]

Later, Drake joined forces with a French pirate named Tetsu and his small crew, and a band of escaped Spanish slaves, known as the Cimaroon. They ambushed a Spanish mule train of 190 animals loaded with gold and silver and headed for the treasure house at Nombre de Dios. Their seized booty has been estimated to have been nearly fifteen tons in silver ingots and 100,000 British pounds in gold coins.[33]

Since England and Spain had signed a peace treaty during Drake's absence, he and his crew were technically pirates. As a result, Drake was forced to go into hiding for nearly two years before receiving Queen Elizabeth's pardon.[34]

On December 13, 1577, Francis Drake, on board the *Pelican* (soon to be renamed the *Golden Hind*), and four other English ships set sail on a secret expedition against Spanish interests along the Pacific Coast of the Americas.[35] In 1578 Drake passed through the Strait of Magellan and reached the waters of the Pacific. Unfortunately, he had lost all of the other members of his small fleet, and as a consequence, the *Golden Hind* was now operating on its own.[36]

The *Golden Hind* sailed northward along South America's Pacific coast, plundering numerous Spanish vessels and ports. The biggest prize of all was the treasure ship *Cacafuego*, whose cargo supposedly included 80 pounds of gold, 13 chests of royals of plate, a large quantity of precious gems, and 26 tons of silver.[37]

Given the general alarm among the Spanish fomented by Drake's numerous conquests along the Pacific Coast, the *Golden Hind* was now the primary focus of every Spanish naval vessel in Drake's path. Therefore, he abandoned his privateering mission and headed west for the comparative safety of the Pacific Ocean. According to David Cordingly:[38]

> He miraculously survived storms, attacks by hostile islanders, and the grounding of his ship on a coral reef among the islands of Indonesia, and arrived back at Plymouth on September 26, 1580, after a voyage lasting two years and nine months."

When Drake sailed into Plymouth, he became the first Englishman and the second man ever after the Portuguese navigator Ferdinand Magellan to circumnavigate the world.[39] Queen Elizabeth, who authorized him to take 10,000 British pounds for himself and another 8,000 pounds for his crew, later knighted him on board the Golden Hind in recognition of his exploits.[40]

War was declared between Spain and England in 1585, and Sir Francis played an important role in the conflict from its onset. After again sailing to the New World, he ravaged the ports of Santo Domingo, Hispaniola and Cartagena, Venezuela, and then captured the Fort of San Augustine, Florida, on his return to England.[41]

In 1585 the Spanish sent a massive Armada to attack England and end British interference with the Spanish domination of the world's sea-lanes once and for all. Drake was the vice admiral of the English fleet, and second in overall command to Lord Howard of Effingham at the time of the Spanish invasion. Along with extreme weather conditions, Drake played a significant part in the destruction of the Spanish Armada in 1588. He continued his tormenting of Spain until the end of his career, when he contracted dysentery off the coast of Panama, and died on January 27, 1596.[42] Celebration and jubilation throughout the Spanish Empire upon the news of his death rivaled the intense mourning that occurred in England.

Chapter Three: Sir Henry Morgan, King of Pirates

*L*ike so many other pirates or privateers of his day, little is known about Morgan's early life. Even the exact date and place of his birth have been subject to dispute. Historians say that he was born in 1635 in either Penkarne (Monmouth, England) or Llanrhymny (Glamorgan, Wales) into a Welsh farming family. He remained in relative obscurity until 1654-55,[43] when he joined a large army of 8000-9000 troops authorized by Oliver Cromwell and commanded by General Venables. The army was commissioned to invade the Spanish in Barbados. It is unclear whether Morgan was a volunteer or, as is more commonly believed, joined the army to escape his condition as an indentured servant on the Island. In that era it was a common practice to kidnap individuals from somewhere else and transport them to Barbadous where they were forced into servitude.[44]

In spite of the impressive size of his army and the support of a large naval force under the leadership of Admiral Penn, Venables' attack on the city of Santa Domingo was soundly defeated, and the surviving British troops had to flee. Venables' forces next invaded the then largely unpopulated and economically insignificant island of Jamaica. Not surprisingly, they overran its 200 Spanish defenders and converted it into a new British colony.[45] "Lord Protector" Cromwell, who had much greater expectations of his large and costly army, was not amused! When Venables and Admiral Penn returned to England, he had them imprisoned in the Tower of London as a reward for their services.[46]

Meanwhile, Henry Morgan persisted in Jamaica, surviving both disease and the attacks of Spanish rebels, which, collectively, had a significant impact on the size of the occupying British force. In 1662 he was appointed a military officer and also received his commission as a privateer.[47] Two years later he set sail for Central America with a small squadron of ships. Much of his effort there was devoted to plundering the three Spanish settlements of Villa Hermosa, Trujillo, and Gran Granada, the Nicaraguan silver mining capitol.[48] In attacking these three settlements, he certainly at least broke the spirit of his Letter of Marque, since it is unlikely that the document made any provisions for the conquest of enemy cities. Such actions were usually regarded as acts of piracy.

He returned to Jamaica to find that his uncle, Sir Edward Morgan, had been appointed Commander of all British forces in the West Indies. Henry, now a wealthy man because of his accumulated plunder, married his uncle's daughter, Mary Elizabeth, in early 1665 and began investing heavily in local plantations.[49]   He also developed a close friendship with the Jamaican Governor, Thomas Modyford.[50]

In 1666 Henry Morgan was named Colonel of the Militia at Port Royal, Jamaica. Upon the death of Edward Mansvelt (or Mansfield), Dutch leader of the privateer/pirate association known as Brethren of the Coast, Morgan was elected by the association's members to fill Mansvelt's place as well. Thus, within a one-year period, Morgan became one of the most powerful military figures in the West Indies.[51]

The following year, Britain and Spain signed a non-aggression pact, which would have seemed to bring Morgan's privateering days to an end. However, Governor Modyford feared that the Spanish might be taking advantage of the lull in hostilities and secretly planning an invasion of Jamaica. Therefore, in January 1668 Modyford ordered Morgan "…to draw together the English privateers and take prisoners of the Spanish nation, whereby you may gain information of that enemy".[52]

Morgan assembled a fleet of roughly ten ships and 500 crewmembers, and then set sail for southern Cuba. Upon reaching Cuba he was joined by a band of French pirates from Tortuga. Realizing that his combined force was still insufficient to launch a successful attack on Havana, he marched his men 30 miles inland and captured the smaller but affluent town of Puerto del Principe. It is rumored that Morgan, after overwhelming the town's defenders, imprisoned the survivors in a local church where they were tortured until ransomed for 50,000 pieces of eight.[53]

Disappointed by the size of the booty, the French buccaneers departed. Morgan, however, sailed his remaining fleet to the Isthmus of Panama and the city of Puerto Bello on its northern coast. Puerto Bello was a critical port, since it was the main departure point from which treasure ships sailed for Spain. Three major forts protected Puerto Bello because of its obvious importance to the Spanish empire. Morgan landed his crew outside of Puerto Bello and launched his attack by canoe under cover of darkness. The forts fell to Morgan's vicious attacks on July 11-12, 1668.[54] Castle San Geronimo put up a heated resistance until Morgan is rumored to have formed a human shield made up of nuns, other women, and old men in front of his forces for the final attack. Once the Port was under his control, he is also said to have repulsed a relief army of 3,000 troops sent by the Governor of Panama. He again ransomed the city and returned to Jamaica in August, 250,000 pieces of eight richer than when he left.[55] He was now a tremendously wealthy man.

Although Henry Morgan had won the admiration of many Englishmen with his exploits against the Spanish, he had technically exceeded the terms of his privateering commission. Fortunately for Morgan, an Admiralty Court convened in March of 1669 declared that his capture of Puerto Bello was legitimate.[56] While his crew celebrated the decision and squandered their shares of the booty in the taverns of Port Royal, Morgan bought up more local plantations.

In April of 1669 Morgan's actions gave rise to what many regard as his finest hour when he and his fleet of 8-9 ships and approximately 600 men found themselves on Lake Maracaibo in Venezuela.[57] Even though Morgan had easily captured the partially deserted city of Maracaibo and extracted a modest ransom from its residents to keep him from putting the city to the torch, he was unable to escape with his booty. His Spanish adversary, Vice Admiral Alonso del Campo y Espinosa, had placed three large men-of-war, any one of which was capable of destroying Morgan's entire fleet, at the mouth of the lake's narrow channel to the sea, thereby blocking Morgan's escape. The vice admiral himself was in command of the largest of the warships, the 48-gun *Magdalena*. Between the Spanish and English fleets was an enemy fortress whose cannons were trained on the water.

Morgan broke the military standoff on May 1 by offering the Spanish an opportunity to surrender. When the Spaniards laughingly refused, Morgan executed yet another clever ruse. He selected one of his sloops, cut several additional gun ports into her sides, inserted cannon-like logs into them, and crewed the vessel with log dummies dressed in sailors' clothing. He loaded this disguised sloop with kegs of gunpowder, coated it with tar, and had twelve volunteers sail it into the midst of the Spanish fleet. The Spanish vice admiral apparently decided to wait until the sloop pulled up beside the *Magdalena* so that it could be sunk with a single devastating broadside. He finally realized that he had been deceived when the twelve English volunteers suddenly attached their vessel to the Spanish man-of-war with grappling hooks, lit the short fuses on the kegs, and jumped overboard. Although the vice admiral managed to escape, the *Magdalena* exploded, while a second Spanish man-of-war was burned down to its hull. In the ensuing confusion, Morgan easily captured the remaining enemy warship. Morgan is reputed to have recovered another 15,000 pieces of eight as well as gold bullion from the sunken men-of-war. Afterwards, he turned his attention to the vice admiral's bastion. Morgan sailed to the fortress and launched a number of longboats filled with pirates toward the shore in apparent preparation for a nighttime land invasion. With darkness ensuing, observers within the Spanish stronghold could not see that Morgan's men lay down flat in the longboats and returned to their ships.[58,59] So deceived, the fort's defenders redirected their guns from facing the water to facing the land in order to repel the anticipated attack. No longer in danger from the fortress, Morgan and his fleet then sailed out the mouth of the lake and returned to Jamaica. As usual, Morgan's men drank in celebration of their victories while he invested.

A month after Morgan's return to Jamaica, Governor Modyford was forced to announce that England and Spain were at peace. However, he soon concluded that a few small raids conducted by Spanish dissidents after the declaration of peace were sufficient justification for him to order a massive retaliation against the enemy he so distrusted. According to Konstam[60] "...he gave Morgan ambiguous orders...allowing him 'to doe and performe all matter of Explolts which may tend to the Preservation and Quiett of Jamayca.'" Morgan responded by proclaiming a general call to arms.

In December of 1670, he and 1,800–2,000 English and French privateers/pirates set sail for Panama in a fleet of 33-36 ships to initiate what Konstam[61] characterizes as "...one of the largest battles fought in the Americas before the start of the 18th century."

Morgan and his men landed at the mouth of the Chagres River, quickly overran the fort of San Lorenzo which had been erected to protect the waterway, canoed up the river and cut through a dense jungle to confront the Spanish in front of the city of Panama. While the defending forces were similar in size to Morgan's army, they offered little resistance to the attackers. Even the barrier created by a herd of 2,000 cattle strategically situated in front of the defenders failed to serve as a deterrent. After capturing the city, Morgan and his men were said to have extracted some 400,000 pieces-of-eight from its residents, razed the city, and returned to Jamaica.[62]

The Spanish Crown wasted no time in putting pressure on the British to live up to the terms of their peace treaty. It was clear to all that Governor Modyford had exceeded his authority when he activated Morgan and his fleet. By June, Modyford was under arrest. He was sent to England and imprisoned for two years in the Tower of London.[63] Morgan was also summoned to London where a similar fate may well have awaited him. However, he quickly made a number of powerful friends and so charmed King Charles II that five years after Morgan initiated his attack on Panama, the King had Morgan knighted for his exploits.[64]

Morgan, now Sir Henry, returned to Jamaica and lived the life of a wealthy sugar planter. He served for some time as the Lieutenant Governor, played an active role in ridding the area of pirates, and died on August 25, 1688, at the age of 53.[65]

Chapter Four: The Evolution of the Jolly Roger

$\mathcal{T}$he latter part of the seventeenth century marked the dawn of the Golden Age of Piracy and the evolution of pirate flags, which are usually grouped under the general heading of the "Jolly Roger". Many feel that the name was derived from the French term "jolie rouge", sarcastically interpreted as pretty red. It stems from the use of red flags in both army and naval battles of the 1600's and 1700's to signal that no quarter would be given unless the other combatant agreed to unconditional surrender. Failure to comply immediately guaranteed the opponent that he faced no quarter or certain death if he lost the ensuing battle. In 1694, the British Crown even enacted a law that required each of its privateers to fly a red flag that had a Union Jack in the upper left hand corner -- a red jack, as it was commonly known.[66] The basis for this legal requirement may have been to differentiate British privateers from British naval vessels by the flying of distinctly different ensigns.

Later, pirates developed a preference for black flags, black being a color traditionally associated with death, featuring a human skull or a skull and crossed bones. The skull or skull and crossed bones had long been used as religious symbols for death. Crucifixes of that era often displayed a skull and crossed bones beneath Christ's feet to reflect his triumph over death. Also, remember that the Greek name for the site of Christ's crucifixion, Golgotha, means Place of the Skull.

Several of the better-known pirates are thought to have personalized their ensigns' designs, so that their intended victims would be aware of exactly whom they were about to face. The hope was that these intended victims might be so terrified by the knowledge of the identity of their specific attacker that they would surrender without a single shot being fired. Personalization involved the use of a number of different symbols to evoke fear. We have already seen that a skull or a skull and crossed bones were employed to symbolize death. An entire skeleton implied that a tormented death lay just ahead.[67] Blackbeard's addition of horns to his skeleton was likely nothing more than a further reference to the devil, his oft-assumed partner. Again, according to Miller Pope,[68] a dart or spear was used to indicate a violent death, and a bleeding heart a slow and painful death. A raised hand or arm holding a dagger or sword suggested a general willingness to kill you, while an hourglass said that your time to live was fleeting. Sandra MacLean Clunies and Bruce Roberts suggest that the term Jolly Roger may, instead, have been "… derived from 'Old Roger,' [an English] nickname for the devil."[69]

Surely, any seaman who saw a black Jolly Roger hoisted on an approaching armed vessel would certainly have been alarmed, perhaps even panicked. However, the display of a red Jolly Roger would undoubtedly make his blood run cold. Such a sight was a guarantee that if defeated in the upcoming struggle, his fate was could only be death.

Yet, just how likely was a merchant seaman to ever encounter a red Jolly Roger in actual combat? Unfortunately, our knowledge of the personalization of Jolly Rogers, particularly ones with a bold red background, is probably even less well documented than the early lives of some of our most notorious buccaneers. What may be likely is that the actual sighting of a red Jolly Roger was probably an exceedingly rare event, bordering on the non-existent.

As is the case with almost any aspect of the study of Pirates of the Golden Age, there are widely varying views and opinions on the subject of their flags. For example, John Matthews[70] states, "...several pirates flew red flags rather than the more familiar black-and-white skull and crossbones." If his assertion is correct, who were these pirates flying red Jolly Rogers?

The only illustration that Matthews uses in support of his contention is definitely an intriguing one. In his two-page section on "Ships and Flags", Matthews shows the personalized Jolly Roger of Henry "Long Ben" Avery, which is commonly believed to have consisted of a skull and crossbones with the skull wearing a do rag or head scarf and facing to the right. Matthews depicts the flag with a black background, as it is in most illustrations. On the opposite page under the title "Pirate Flags", however, he shows the same flag with a striking red background. The reason that this illustration is so interesting is that if one were to pick any pirate to give no quarter to his intended victims out of all those whom we have or will discuss, it might well be "Long Ben" Avery.

Chapter six describes how Avery (1695) captured the *Gang-i-sawai*, an Indian treasure vessel, after a hard fought and prolonged battle. Avery's treatment of the Indian crew and passengers is likely to remain forever among the most brutal ever inflicted upon pirate captives.[71] His action would certainly seem to reflect the kind of pirate who would fly a red Jolly Roger and give no quarter to any victim who resisted his attack.

Christopher Moody, whose career remains shrouded in obscurity, is the one pirate whose name has traditionally been linked with the flying of a red Jolly Roger. He is believed to have once crewed with both Bartholomew "Black Bart" Roberts and Edward "Blackbeard" Teach. One source even suggests that he may have been present when Black Bart attacked the island of Principe and when Blackbeard blockaded the port of Charles Town (Charleston, SC).[72]

In any event, Moody's flag is generally assumed to have a red background, indicating that he would give no quarter as has already been noted. On the extreme left was depicted a golden hour glass with blue wings, which essentially informed the viewer that he or she had very little time left in their life once they could see the emblem. In the center was a white arm holding a white sword or dagger. This symbol was very similar to that purportedly flown by Thomas Tew. As already discussed, its implied message was that "we are ready to kill you". On the right-hand side of the flag was a golden skull and crossed bones, which of course connoted death.[73] Taken collectively, the color of the flag and the various symbols displayed upon it did not auger well for an intended victim's future.

Thus, it seems that the answer to the question posed above is that there were probably no more than one or two pirates who flew a red Jolly Roger: namely Christopher Moody and/or "Long Ben" Avery. Though we have little reliable information on record about either of them, what we do know would certainly seem to indicate that each would make a good candidate for flying a red Jolly Roger,

Coincidently, my wife and I have recently returned from a three-day trip to Charleston, SC, where we stayed with friends on their boat. One day we had lunch at a restaurant called The Buccaneer, where the food and service were exceptional, and the décor was beyond belief. On every wall filling every available space hung a museum quality collection of seventeenth and eighteenth century pirate artifacts. The owner, Anthony E. Bakker, sold his fascinating book entitled *Charleston & The Golden Age of Piracy*[73] in the restaurant. In his book on p. 19,[74] I discovered that Christopher Moody, the shadowy pirate who supposedly participated in Blackbeard's blockade of Charleston, had apparently attempted to blockade the city once again in late October of 1718 with his ship the *Eagle* and a companion pirate sloop. When the South Carolina Governor, Robert Johnson, ordered an attack on the two pirate ships on November 5, the *Eagle* escaped but its pirate companion was overrun. Later in the day the *Eagle* was sighted again, and a fierce struggle ensued. When fighting ceased and the *Eagle* was finally boarded, it was found that many of her occupants, consisting of male prisoners and female indentured servants bound for London as well as the pirate crew, were dead. However, Moody had apparently been warned of the impending attempt to capture him by sympathizers in Charleston and made good his escape before the battle was initiated. That same year Moody was captured, tried, convicted, and hanged at Cape Coast Castle in Cabo Corso, Ghana (now Cape Coast, Ghana).[75]

I made another exciting discovery at lunch as well. Hanging on one wall of personalized pirate Jolly Roger replicas was Charles Vane's ensign, which I had never before seen. What made it particularly exciting was that it portrayed a rightward facing skull with a yellow do rag staring at a white dagger offset by a bright red background! So, my boldly proclaimed assumption that only two pirates at most ever flew a red personalized Jolly Roger is undoubtedly subject to question. Once you read Charles Vane's story, you'll quickly realize why he was also such a fitting candidate for flying a red Jolly Roger.

In making a final check on the accuracy of my endnotes, I came across a web site that I had never before encountered. It is a British web source; Bonaventure: org.uk/ed/flags.him. I was trying to verify some specifics about my favorite pirate Stede Bonnet's personalized Jolly Roger. After searching the web for the appropriate information, I encountered one reference called *Pirate Mythtory...Pirate Flags* by an uncited author that was extremely thought provoking.

In his article, the author claims that most of the web's descriptions of the personalized Jolly Rogers of the Golden Age, including a number by well-established historians, are unverified at best. He goes on to assert that many are actually incorrect, often being based on an undated, unreferenced manuscript in the National Maritime Museum. He further asserts that at least twenty of the best-known personalized Jolly Rogers fall into this category. He also claims that he has verified the design of over 100 personalized Jolly Rogers, which he intends to post on a future web site. Three interesting examples of his research are given below. In contrast to my discussion of Henry Avery, he asserts that the do ragged, rightward facing skull on either a black or red background may not be authentic. To support his claim, he states that neither do rags nor earrings were likely to have been seen on pirates prior to the 1880s -- long after Avery's demise -- when they were popularized in the famous buccaneer paintings of Howard Pyle. The most striking example of a personalized Jolly Roger that he attempts to discredit is that of Edward Teach, or Blackbeard. First he claims that there is no "period source" that supports this most famous of all Jolly Rogers. He also has serious doubts about the horns shown on Blackbeard's skeleton, which he feels "...render it unlikely from a stylistic prospective". Finally, he notes that "Blackbeard's flag is described in at least one Colonial Office document as a 'Death's Head'" rather than an entire skeleton. He also employs this same argument to cast doubt on Stede Bonnet's personalized flag. He notes that in the *Boston Newsletter* of June 1716 it is described as a death's head. In this instance at least noting that Steed's ensign depicted a death's head would not necessarily seem to be at odds with the usual depiction presented in most books on pirates.

As stated before, much of what we know about the Golden Age pirates is based on oral history, tradition, or myth. So, it seems clear that the debate about these fascinating individuals and the details involved in their often-short lives will go on and on.

Stede Bonnett

George Lawther

Christopher Moody

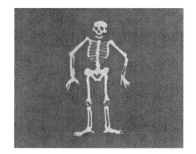

Edward Low

Blackbeard

Richard Worley

Charles Vane

Thomas Tew

Chapter Five: Thomas Tew, the Rhode Island Pirate

Thomas Tew and Gov. Fletcher

*M*any authorities agree that Thomas Tew was most likely born in Maidford, Northhamptonshire, England. Although the date of his birth is unknown, Paul Orton[76] is writing a fascinating and detailed history of Tew. By a series of careful calculations, Orton estimates that Tew had to have been born no later than the 1650's. According to Orton, who may be a multi-generations-removed descendent of the infamous pirate, Tew claimed to trace his lineage to the Tews (Richard Tew and Mary Clarke) of Rhode Island, who had immigrated to America in 1640. He appears to have come from a well to do background. It is generally believed that he came to the United States as a child (possibly with his parents), where he lived in Newport, Rhode Island. He eventually married and had two daughters.

The Golden Age of Piracy is commonly recognized as having begun in approximately 1690. It is interesting that the Thomas Tew family chose that time frame (1690-1692) to leave their home in America for Bermuda. Some authors believe that when Tew arrived in Bermuda, he already had or quickly acquired the reputation of being a pirate. In any event, by 1692 his strong inclination towards piracy clearly expressed itself. Together with a number of prominent Bermuda backers, he acquired a 70-ton, heavily armed sloop, the *Amity,* with the ostensive purpose of acting as a privateer under a Letter of Marque from Governor Ritchier.[77] Under the terms of the contract, his main mission was to attack a French factory located at Goree in Gambia on coastal West Africa.[78] While Tew was to have been accompanied by another sloop of the Royal African Company of London, the two ships soon separated in a storm.

Once Tew was free of his fellow captain, he assembled his entire crew and addressed them concerning their mission. He pointed out that attacking a French factory in West Africa would be of little if any benefit to them personally. Instead, he proposed that they become pirates, set sail for the Red Sea, and seek out rich merchant ships to attack, capture, and plunder. His crew and officers are said to have responded with a cry of "A gold Chain or a wooden Leg, we'll stand by you".[79] Tew quickly drew up code or contract that ignored the issue of which national flags could be attacked. However, it went into great detail about the distribution of any booty "...that shall bee ffound, Taken, Gotten, had or Recovered at any time or place in any mannor dureing the whole term of the said voyage or voyages or Expedition.[80] While not necessarily up to modern standards of spelling or English grammar, the agreement clearly dispelled any claims to privateering instead of pirating on Tew's part. After signing the agreement, the crew and captain sailed to the Cape of Good Hope, and eventually traveled on to the Red Sea.

Tew's personal pirate flag is reported by many authors to have been a raised arm holding a sword (in white) on a black background. Symbolically, the flag conveyed the message "we are ready to kill you".[81]

While the *Amity crew* sailed for many months with nothing to show for their efforts, Tew's men apparently never lost faith in their captain.[82] He responded to this faith with his fearless leadership when the pirates came upon a small fleet of six Indian merchant ships, the leader and largest of which was protected by 300-500 Indian soldiers. When Tew first proposed attacking the leading merchantman, his crew expressed strong reservations about facing such overwhelming odds. Tew assured them that the enemy soldiers would be poorly equipped and trained, and offer little if any resistance. His emboldened crew followed his lead and quickly overwhelmed the Indian vessel while incurring no serious wounds or loss of life.[83]   After the battle, they found that they had captured a vast treasure -- 100,000 pounds in gold and silver alone, not to mention the remainder of the extensive treasure cargo.   According to their signed contract or agreement, each crewmember received a share of approximately 1,000 to 3,000 pounds, or one to three million in today's dollars.[84]   Tew as captain earned an even bigger share, immediately elevating him to the status of multimillionaire.   He eventually richly rewarded his Bermuda backers well beyond their initial expectations.

While some of the crew wished to return to America, the ship's quartermaster and twenty-three members of the crew decided to leave the *Amity* and to remain in Madagascar to enjoy their newfound riches.   What occurred next to Tew and his remaining crew is even sketchier than the usual stories of the Golden Age pirates.   In fact, all of the details concerning his return voyage are dependent on one source according to Orton –– a source that has been repeatedly challenged over time. (See the discussion at the end of this Chapter).   That source is entitled *The General History of the Robberies and Murders of the Most Notorious Pyrates, written* by Captain Charles Johnson and published on May 4, 1724.

According to Orton/Johnson, on the return voyage Tew and his men supposedly encountered the ship *Victoire*, captained by a presumably notorious French pirate named Misson or Mission.   Orton readily admits that he has found little or no independent verification of Captain Misson's activities.   Nevertheless, he states that Johnson claims Captain Misson had established an extremely well armed pirate colony called Libertatia, the "Republic of the Seas", on the coast of Madagascar.[85]

Orton claims that it was governed quite democratically on strict republican principles a century before the French revolution took place.   Tew was invited to visit, perhaps even join, the colony; and impressed by both the fortifications and manner of government, he did so.   He became a member of the Governing Council, and was soon made Admiral of Libertatia.

Zepke[86] claims that Tew strongly recommended increasing the population of Libertatia to make it more capable of defending itself from attack.   He is supposed to have spent several months sailing in search of Indian merchantmen in order to recruit new citizens from the passengers and crews for the colony.   Then, when he and Misson were each involved in separate missions away from Libertitia with portions of their crews, Tew received word that the Colony had been overrun by local natives.   Apparently, most of its inhabitants were slaughtered, including the members of Tew's forces who had remained behind.   Tew decided to return to Rhode Island and asked his good friend Misson to accompany him.   Misson agreed to go together with him at least as far as Europe, and they departed in separate sloops. Early in their voyage, a severe storm arose; and while Tew struggled to keep his sloop afloat, Misson and his entire crew were lost right before Tew's eyes. Tew and his men then proceeded in shock to America.[87]

Interestingly, Orton points out that many researchers doubt the very existence of Captain Charles Johnson and regard Libertatia as fictional. He goes on to note that some believe the author of this fictional journal was in fact the internationally known writer Daniel Defoe, who is more frequently associated with his popular novel *Robinson Crusoe*. The authorship issue continued to be debated until 1932, when the American scholar John Robert Moore, the most renowned expert on Defoe of his era according to Orton, championed the "Defoe cause" at a literary meeting. He is even said to have devoted eight years to persuading many of the world's libraries containing a copy of Johnson's history to re-catalogue it under the name of Daniel Defoe. However, in 1998 Furbank and Owens basically destroyed Moore's theory in a work sarcastically entitled *The Canonization of Daniel Defoe.*[88] When one considers that Johnson's history is the primary source of our knowledge about Mary Reed and Anne Bonny, as well as many other Golden Age pirates, questions of its authorship and authenticity become of obvious importance.

Tew returned to Newport, Rhode Island, where his ill-gotten but immense wealth assured him ready access to society and the world of commerce. He is said to have established separate shipping lines for trade with Madagascar in New York, Pennsylvania, North Carolina and Rhode Island.[89] His business travels to New York even allowed him to develop a close personal relationship with the state's governor, Ben Fletcher.

Tew's retirement from piracy was to be short lived, since numerous potential backers pressured him almost continuously to try to repeat the success of his first buccaneering adventure. Therefore, seven to eight months after his return, he purchased another privateering commission or Letter of Marque from his good friend, Governor Fletcher, fitted out another sloop also called the *Amity,* and set sail for the Red Sea.[90]

When he and his crew reached the mouth of the Red Sea in August of 1695, Tew joined forces with the notorious Henry "Long Ben" Avery and several other pirates in pursuit of a 25-ship fleet of Indian merchantmen. The *Amity* attacked a merchantman believed to be the *Fateh Muhammed.* Though Tew had expected little resistance, a ferocious battle ensued. According to Johnson/Orton, early in the fray "...a shot carried away the Rim of Tew's Belly, who held his Bowels with his hands" for several seconds before dropping dead on the deck.[91] His stunned crew quickly surrendered and was taken prisoner by the Indians. They were later supposedly freed when the *Fateh Muhammed* was captured by Captain Avery.

During his brief career, Tew succeeded in reaping a considerable fortune and even escaping the hangman's noose that was the fate of so many of his Golden Age contemporaries. Therefore, one cannot help but wonder why he was so willing to give up the "good life" and return to his extremely dangerous and socially unacceptable profession as a pirate. Golden Age pirates were, indeed, an unusual breed of men.

Chapter Six: Henry "Long Ben" Avery, the Arch Pirate

*H*enry "Long Ben" Avery is certainly one of the more interesting of the Golden Age pirates. While his nickname would suggest a man of towering height, the noted pirate historian David Cordingly characterizes him as being short to "…medium height, rather fat, with a dissolute appearance and what is described as a jolly [presumably red] complexion". [92]

Estimates of his year of birth are variously cited as being between the middle 1650s and 1665 near Plymouth, England. (The famous novelist Daniel Defoe claims the appropriate year to be 1653.[93]) While his father apparently tried to interest his son in academic pursuits at an early age, Henry was extremely wild and would have none of it.[94] Instead, he supposedly ran off to sea and joined the crew of a merchantman. His behavior on board ship was so uncontrollable that the captain is reported to have kept him locked in the ship's hold until he could be put ashore as soon as they reached either North or South Carolina.[95]

Three years later Avery returned to England to find his father dead and his mother dying. Orphaned, he briefly relied on stealing to sustain himself, but soon went back to sea to earn his livelihood.[96] He sailed on a number of merchant ships, and some even suggest that he was involved with the slave trade.[97] By 1694 he was the first mate on the privateer *Charles* under the command of Captain Gibson. One night Gibson retired early after losing a bout with the bottle, only to be awakened from a stupor by Avery in the middle of the night.[98] Avery informed the captain that the ship was under sail and that he had taken command. He also noted that they were headed for Madagascar where he and his followers intended to pursue their fortune. He concluded by telling Gibson that he and the few crewmembers who still supported him were being taken ashore in a small boat.[99]

Upon reaching Madagascar, Avery sent the following notice to England to be posted in British newspapers:[100]

> I was riding her[e] in the *Fancy*, man-of-war, formerly the *Charles* of the Spanish expedition… being then and now a ship of 46 guns, 150 men and bound to seek our fortunes. I have never yet wronged any English or Dutch, nor ever intend whilst I am commander.....If you or any whom you may inform are desirous to know what we are at a distance, then make your ancient [ensign] up in a ball or bundle and hoist him at the mizen peak, the mizen being furled. I shall answer with the same, and never molest you, but my men are hungry, stout, and resolute, and should they exceed my desire I cannot help myself.
>
> As yet an Englishman's friend
> -Henry Avery

Avery's bold notice left little doubt as to his intentions, even towards his own countrymen. He soon forged an alliance with another well-known pirate captain of the day, Thomas Tew, and began patrolling the seas between India and the Middle East in search of Indian treasure fleets. In September 1695, Avery and his fellow pirates came upon two treasure ships of the Indian Grand Mogul on their way home from their annual trading expedition to Arabia. The buccaneers quickly overcame the smaller of the two vessels, the *Fatah Mohammed*; but the struggle to subdue *the Gang-i-Sawai*, the flagship of the Grand Mogul's treasure fleet, was fierce and prolonged.[101] The *Gang-i-Sawai* had over 600 passengers, including members of the royal family and court, and a treasure in gold, silver and jewels that would be worth over $105,000,000 - $400,000,000 in today's market place.[102]

Once the pirates secured victory, the mayhem that occurred on board the *Gang-i-Sawai* may be unparalleled in buccaneer history. First the male passengers and crew were tortured to determine if any knew of treasure hidden onboard the ship; then they were hacked into pieces and their remains thrown overboard. Next, the female passengers, including the Grand Mogul's own daughter, were raped repeatedly until the pirates tired of them. Finally, depending on which account one chooses to believe, the ravaged females were abandoned on a deserted island, thrown overboard by the pirates, or committed suicide by jumping overboard.[101-103] Since any raped female was considered to be unsuitable for marriage under Muslim law, it is likely that some combination of the latter two theories best describes the fate of the unfortunate women.

The Grand Mogul was outraged by the pirates' actions and banned any trade with the East India Company until Great Britain brought all of the pirates responsible to justice. The British Government and the East India Company pooled their efforts and posted a reward of 1500 pounds for the capture of Avery and his crew.[104]

Avery and his crew first learned of their predicament when they sailed to New Providence, Bahamas. After failing to buy their pardon from the Governor, the pirates divided their treasure and fled. Some went to England, where most were caught and hanged. Avery's fate depends on your source of information. Cordingly, who seems to views him as being less cruel than many other historians, also sees him as one of the few pirates who realized when it was time to retire from his buccaneering career. He cites what he terms as the popular view that he escaped to a tropical island where he lived in comfort until the end of his days. In contrast, his own personal view is that Avery sailed to Dublin where he was swindled by local merchants out of his share of the *Gang-i-Sawai* booty and died in poverty.[105] Zepke also notes that there are stories that he reached Ireland and remained in hiding, living comfortably off his share of the Grand Mogul's treasure for the remainder of his days. From her perspective, however, the more commonly told version of Avery's fate is that since he had taken his share of the treasure primarily in diamonds; and unable to appear in public for fear of capture, he gave his diamonds to friends to sell for him. When they failed to return to him with the proceeds, he is reported to have died in poverty and been buried in a pauper's grave in Biddiford, England.[106]

Regardless of the real truth about his end, Avery enjoyed tremendous notoriety in his day and attracted many would-be imitators to life on the high seas. As a result, he became known as the "Arch Pirate".

In North Carolina we include state history as part of our fourth grade curriculum. That, of course, involves a significant focus on some of the pirates who terrorized the coastline of the Carolinas during the Golden Age. Since I retired from my first career with the National Institutes of Health, I have read and written fairly extensively on pirates. As a result, I have had the opportunity to give a number of pirate presentations to both children in the classroom and mixed audiences at various pirate festivals.

The first question I was asked by students in one fourth grade classroom was to give the origin of the word "pirate". Naturally, I couldn't answer that question, and was off to a great start with my young audience. (See the definition in the Glossary.) Next, another student asked me about the youngest pirate of the Golden Age. This is an excellent but very difficult question to answer with any degree of accuracy. So little is known about the early lives of even the most notorious pirates usually that we can hazard only a guess as to when a young man or woman actually turned to a life of piracy.

Tradition suggests that Grace O'Malley, the sixteenth century Pirate Queen of Ireland, was probably a preteen when she jumped, screaming in rage, from high up in her father's ship's rigging onto the back of an English pirate who was about to stab him from behind. Anne Bonny may have been only sixteen when she rejected her father's arranged marriage to a prominent Charlestonian, eloped with a common sailor she had recently met on the Charles Town docks, and fled to New Providence, Bahamas, the pirate capital of the western hemisphere. William Kidd went to sea almost certainly as a preteen when he became a crewmember of the pirate ship *Blessed William*. And by the age of eleven, William "Billy" Lewis was sailing out of Boston Harbor under the tutelage of pirate Captain Banister.

My personal candidate for the youngest pirate of the Golden Age would be Henry "Long Ben" Avery. As we saw above, he ran away from home to join the crew of a merchantman at a very young age, perhaps when he was no older than eight or nine. Moreover, I think he was born with the soul of a pirate. In my opinion, he was evil from the very first breath he ever drew on this earth.

Chapter Seven: William Kidd, Unlucky Privateer or Ruthless Pirate?

*W*illiam Kidd was one of the best-known and most controversial pirates of the early Golden Era, and his buried treasure was legendary, remaining so to this very day. It was featured in such famous tales as Edgar Allen Poe's *The Gold-Bug*[107] and is undoubtedly still being pursued by legions of would-be treasure hunters.

As the title of this chapter suggests, Kidd, like many of the pirates who followed in his footsteps, may well have been particularly unlucky. His lack of luck or good fortune and, indeed, his ultimate undoing can primarily be attributed to both his crew and to the unscrupulous behavior of his royal financial backers.

Although details of his early life are scarce, most historians believe that William Kidd was born in Greenock, Scotland, around 1645. His poor minister father died when he was only five years old. While still very young, he fled to the sea to seek his livelihood. According to Zepke[108], he spent his first years as a member of the crew of the pirate ship *Blessed William*. Eventually the *Blessed William* surrendered to the British Navy, and Kidd was among the crewmembers who received a royal pardon, presumably because of his young age and/or in return for his promise to renounce his buccaneering ways.[109]

He next turned to privateering and he served the Crown with bravery and distinction during King William's War in the West Indies.[110] His privateering and, perhaps, occasional pirateering activities in the West Indies and the New York area led to his amassing a substantial sum of money by the time his commission expired. Thereafter, he settled in New York, purchasing a home in a fashionable neighborhood, becoming a successful merchant, and joining the general social scene.[111]

Zepke[112] indicates that in 1688, shortly after commencing his new lifestyle, Kidd met the extremely attractive twenty-year-old socialite, Sarah Cox. She was the wife of a prominent New York alderman and merchant, who fell overboard from his own ship and drowned. Apparently the feelings that were eventually to exist between William and Sarah had not yet fully developed, and she chose another wealthy merchant, John Oort, to become her next husband. However, when he also died in 1691, he was in the ground for only eleven days before Sarah and William were finally wed.

In addition to their shared affection, they also enjoyed considerable wealth that allowed them to circulate freely in the best of society. They were prominent members of Trinity Church, where they and their two daughters, Sarah and Elizabeth, had their own pew.[113] Yet, as Zepke[114] so aptly states, "William Kidd had a restless soul and a darker side that struggled with this puritanical lifestyle." By 1695 he could, or at least he chose, to struggle no longer.

In that year he met fellow Scot, Robert Livingston, who persistently encouraged him to resume his career as a privateer in consortium with a number of royal and wealthy backers or silent partners. Among the most famous were Richard, Earl of Bellomont or Bellamont, Governor of Barbados at the time and soon to be the new Governor of Massachusetts and New York, Lord Chancellor John Somers,[115] and even his Royal Highness William III.

Under the terms of the privateer agreement, Bellomont and his fellow backers would bear most of the costs of building and outfitting a ship for the venture, for which they would receive more than half of all treasure taken. King William signed a Letter of Marque, which entitled Kidd and his crew to capture any pirates (and their booty) they encountered as well as any French vessels they engaged. In return, the King was to receive ten percent of the proceeds from the venture. Finally, Kidd and Livingston were to bear the remainder of the costs involved in preparing for the expedition. As their reward, Kidd, Livingston, and the crew, were to share the remainder of all treasure taken. A critical clause of the agreement stated that Kidd and his fellow privateers were to reimburse the backers for all of their expenses if no treasure was acquired.[116] *Adventure Galley*, which was built in London for this specific mission, was a 34-gun, 300-ton vessel with three massive sails and 32 oars to be used if the ship was becalmed.[117]

A full compliment of crew required 150 sailors. Kidd recruited 70 of the most skilled seamen in London and then set sail for New York where he intended to take care of some personal business and recruit the remainder of his crew. Unfortunately, his first encounter at sea occurred when he passed a British man-of-war, *HMS Duchess,* returning to England. Not only did Kidd refuse to lower his colors in recognition of the man-of-war as tradition required, but his crew also turned away from the man-of-war and repeatedly slapped their backsides. In response to these insults, the British boarded the *Adventure Galley* and impressed many of Kidd's best crewmembers. There has always been a great deal of speculation about what prompted Kidd to behave so outrageously, particularly when he must have known that he would undoubtedly suffer severe consequences for his actions. Most feel that Kidd, like many of his pirate compatriots through the ages, had an extremely large ego and found it very difficult to recognize any authority above his own. He may have been resentful about not being a captain in the Royal Navy himself.[118,119]

Upon reaching New York, he apparently was forced to replenish his recently diminished crew with some of the most undesirable specimens available in the taverns of the city. The *Adventure Galley* set sail from New York on September 5, 1696.[120]

It may well have been Kidd's original intent to follow explicitly the terms of his royal Letter of Marque; i.e., to pursue only pirate ships or those vessels flying the flag of France. On the other hand, some historians feel that given the questionable character of the replacement crew, the majority would be likely to identify closely with any pirates they encountered and had little interest in engaging them in battle. In any event, no pirate prisoners or booty were ever taken. Furthermore, wealthy French merchantmen were few and far between. Therefore, Kidd's standing with the crew, who wanted to capture any ships encountered, regardless of nationality, declined steadily. The situation took on critical proportions when Kidd became involved in a heated argument with dissident crewmember and gunner, William Moore. Kidd hit him in the head with a heavy wooden, metal bound bucket. Moore suffered a serious skull fracture and died the next morning from his wounds.[121] Realizing that he was on the verge of having a mutiny on his hands, Kidd either underwent a total change of heart or, at the very least, significantly broadened his list of potential prey to conform to the wishes of the crew. Shortly thereafter, Kidd, now eighteen months into his mission and essentially empty-handed, encountered a large, presumably French owned, East Indian merchantman, the *Quedagh Merchant*, clearly loaded with a heavy cargo. After a brief struggle Kidd and his crew seized one of the richest treasures of silver, gold, precious jewels and silks ever known in the annals of piracy. Piracy is the most accurate characterization of the event, since the true master of the ship was on board and presented himself to Kidd as an Englishman. Zepke notes than a wealthy Armenian was also on board, and he attempted to ransom the *Quedagh Merchant*. By now Kidd realized that he had crossed a forbidden line, and that his crew would never agree to returning their captured booty because of the legal niceties of a British master versus French ownership, so he merely kept the Armenian's proposed ransom money as well as the captured East Indian treasure.[122]

Suspecting that he would likely face charges of piracy in England, Kidd decided to sail first to New York and seek the support of his backers in return for their share of his fabulous booty. Zepke suggests that he may have stopped and left sizable caches of treasure at Sullivan's Island, South Carolina, Money Island, North Carolina, and Gardiner's Island, off the east end of Long Island,

New York. Estimates of the size of the treasure hoard seized by Kidd and his crew range from 12,000 to 710,000 British pounds.[123] If the upper end of the range is closer to the mark, then Kidd's booty was similar in magnitude to that accumulated by "Long Ben" Avery.

Kidd landed in New York in June of 1699. He quickly sent a lawyer friend, James Emmott, to plead his case with his backer, the newly appointed Governor of New York, Lord Bellomont. To bolster his case, Emmott also took Kidd's royal Letter of Marque as well as a personal letter from Kidd attempting to justify any actions he had taken that were forbidden by the Letter.[124] The Royal Governor appeared to be receptive to Emmott's arguments and urged Kidd to come join him so they could plan his defense. On July 1, Kidd and his family were walking with high hopes up to the entrance of the Governor's mansion in Boston when they were arrested by a contingent of British troops. Up until this moment Kidd was apparently unaware of what a political liability he had become to Bellomont and his other backers. He was immediately sent to London where he was imprisoned at Newgate for two years awaiting his trial His confinement was certainly far from pleasant, since Zepke indicates that Newgate was such a filthy, foul establishment that prisoners often had to be dipped in vinegar just prior to their trials in order to make their body odors more tolerable to others in the courtroom.[125] During his stay, Kidd was denied access to visitors, news, and even pen and paper. He was ill prepared, both physically and mentally, for his trial, which was finally held on May 8-9, 1700.[126] He was charged with several acts of piracy and the murder of William Moore, charges supported by two captured pirates who had formerly been members of his crew. He was quickly found guilty of all charges and sentenced to death by hanging. Upon the rendering of the verdict, Kidd is said to have cried out:

> My Lord, it is a very hard sentence. For my part, I am the innocentest of them all, only I have been sworn against by perjured persons. [127]

Perjured testimony or not, Kidd was taken to Execution Dock on the Thames River to meet his final fate on May 23, 1701. Even the end did not come easily for Kidd. It took nearly two hours to get him through the assembled crowd and onto the gallows. Then, the rope broke the first time before he was finally hanged successfully.[128] His body, bound up in chains, was tarred and displayed over the Thames for several years as a warning to would-be followers.

The execution of
William Kidd

On balance, I feel that the proper answer to the question posed in the title to this Chapter is that William Kidd, while certainly not free from fault, should be viewed as one of the unluckiest of privateers of the Golden Age.

Incidently, Zepke[129] indicates that Kidd's widow, Sarah, was as practical as she was both beautiful and wealthy. In her early thirties, just five months after Kidd's execution, she married her fourth husband, Christopher Rousby.

Chapter Eight: John Redfield, the Unknown Pirate

edfield is perhaps the most obscure of any of the pirates to be considered in this collection of tales. Indeed, little or nothing was really known of him until he joined the crew of the infamous Captain William Kidd. Although he was reputed to have been over six feet tall with a large frame, we are not aware of any sketch or portrait to give some indication of his actual appearance.

Recall that Kidd, fearing retribution at the hands of British justice, decided to return first to New England and plead his case to his backers while offering them their share of his booty. On his return voyage, Kidd is reputed to have anchored off the coast of a small Carolina island near Wilmington in order to make some additional preparations for the future.

Enter John Redfield. Redfield had been a loyal member of Kidd's crew throughout his most recent adventure and had strongly supported Kidd when many of the crew had begun to turn against him prior to the capture of the *Quedagh Merchant*. Furthermore, Redfield was undoubtedly an experienced seaman going back to Queen Anne's War and was clearly Kidd's most trusted confidant and advisor.

Kidd told Redfield that he wanted him to stay behind and keep watch over something for Kidd when he and the rest of the crew departed for Boston. As soon as Redfield agreed to fulfill any mission that Kidd assigned to him, Kidd explained that he was going to bury two iron chests filled with gold and silver on a little island [which has become known as Money Island] that "... lies just south of Bradley Creek Point and immediately east of Shandy Hall opposite the mainland shoreline".[130] The chests were buried that night, and a sapling was planted over each chest to mark the location of the buried treasure. Kidd also instructed Redfield that if five years went by without his hearing from Kidd, he should dig up one of the chests and remove half of its contents for himself. If another five years went by without any attempt at contact, he should dig up the remaining chest and remove half of its contents as well. If anyone other than Kidd were to appear and try to claim the buried treasure in Kidd's name, he would have to show an agreed upon recognition signal in order to have his claim honored. Finally, Kidd gave Redfield a thousand pounds in British gold in return for his loyal services. Once they returned to the pirate ship, Kidd assigned four of his best crewmen to remain behind in support of Redfield; and the next day he sailed to Albemarle Sound, NC, where he acquired a small schooner for Redfield and his men before going on to Boston.[131]

The four crewmen built a residence for Redfield on the mainland but soon tired of the lack of human companionship in the unsettled wilderness. In company with Redfield, they made several trips to the nearest populated site, Charleston, South Carolina, in the small schooner provided to them by Captain Kidd before his departure.[132]

As a result of these short trips, Redfield acquired a wife, and the four crewmen renewed their appetites for their former lifestyles.[133] For the next year and a half, Redfield and his wife enjoyed a bucolic existence. In the spring of the second year, a ship was seen off the coast flying Kidd's ensign. When a small boat was dispatched from the ship and approached the mainland, Kidd was nowhere to be seen. But Redfield did immediately recognize the man in charge of the boat as Max Brisbau, a former shipmate who had also sailed with Captain Kidd.[134] After greeting each other warmly, the two adjourned to Redfield's house for a drink and additional discussion;[135] the remaining pirates went outside the house in order to allow the two captains some privacy for talking. Once the two were alone, Brisbau told Redfield that he had been sent by Captain Kidd to reclaim his treasure.[136] Since Brisbau was unable to furnish Kidd's previously agreed upon recognition signal to verify his claim, Redfield refused to tell where the treasure was buried. Following what was assuredly a heated argument and perhaps even a physical struggle, Redfield's men returned with Brisbau's crew. Redfield was startled to discover that his colleagues had switched their allegiance to Brisbau in order to gain a share of Kidd's buried treasure, which they had just heard about for the first time.[137] Redfield and his wife were taken prisoner and may have been abused for some time in an unsuccessful attempt to induce them to reveal the location of Kidd's buried treasure.[138]

Finally, an exasperated Brisbau and his expanded crew took the two on board his ship and threatened to drown them.[139] Their lives were spared, however, when Charleston Port Authorities who suspected them of smuggling stopped their ship, and all aboard were taken prisoner on suspicion of piracy as well. The Redfields told their story, minus reference to Captain Kidd's treasure, and were released. They took up residence in Charleston and soon were embraced by local society as a successful merchant and his wife.[140] Brisbau and his companions were threatened with prison but eventually released to disappear forever into the annals of pirate history.

While Redfield[141] may never have disturbed Kidd's buried treasure even after learning of Kidd's gruesome death on the gallows at Execution Dock, hundreds, perhaps thousands of others have certainly tried to find it for themselves. Nor is this the only area in which Kidd's treasure has been sought. Susan Block[142] made the following observation in her article on "Money Island":

> Christine Svenningsen, the widow of a party-supply mogul, recently spent $33 million buying up tiny islands in Long Island Sound where Kidd is also rumored to have buried treasure. Though Ms. Svenningsen refuses to divulge her interest in the Thimble Islands, national news media have speculated she might be preparing for a dig.

The most appealing story of searches for Kidd's buried treasure goes back to Money Island and is again reported by Susan Block.[143] She tells of a one-time occupant of Redfield's home in Charleston, named Dr. George Worth, who became a missionary to China. Every five years he was given the opportunity to return to the States on extended leave. He prepared carefully for each visit, writing to the children of his friends and relatives both frightening and, in particular, delighting them with tales of Kidd and his buried treasure. Shortly before each of his returns to the United States, he would send the children in question a treasure map with an accompanying note that the treasure could only be sought on a particular date, which was always chosen to be the night of a full moon. When he returned to the States, he would purchase candy, trinkets, and various foreign coins and bury them at the sight indicated on his map. Then he would take all of the children on a treasure hunt, burning the memory of Captain Kidd and his treasure forever into their young minds.

Chapter Nine: Samuel "Black Sam" Bellamy, the Prince of Pirates

$\mathcal{S}$amuel or "Black Sam" Bellamy was born in the latter part of the 1600's (probably in 1689) in Devonshire, England.[144] Like so many youths from that area, he very likely learned the seafaring trade at an early age. His nickname of "Black Sam" was attributed to his tendency to wear his long black hair in a ponytail.[145]

Most of the authors who deal with his story suggest that both he and his crew were exceptionally courteous to any victims they encountered, which gave rise to another nickname for him: "The Prince of Pirates". This apparent and unusual thoughtfulness seems to be somewhat at odds with the fact that when he left for America to pursue his fortune, he totally abandoned his wife and child in Canterbury.[146]

Bellamy migrated to the United States in 1715, settling in New England and the Cape Cod area. He was searching for adventure and a life on the sea. Instead, he found his true love in the reputedly beautiful fifteen-year-old Maria Hallet of Eastam Harbor, Massachusetts.[147] While tradition suggests that Maria's parents were opposed to the romance since Bellamy was perceived as being well below Maria's social station, the two lovers were undeterred in their affection for each other. It seems likely that Maria was unaware of Bellamy's wife and child back home in England.

To earn support for his lover, respect from her parents, and to respond to his inner need for adventure, Samuel joined the hordes of seamen flocking to Florida to seek instant wealth in the "Gold Rush of 1715". The so-called gold rush was brought about by the sinking of a fleet of Spanish treasure vessels in a widely scattered area along the Florida coast.[148] Before departing for Florida, "Black Sam" enlisted the support of various local friends and backers, chief among whom was Palgrave Williams, a middle-aged, well-to-do goldsmith from a distinguished New England family.[149] Shortly after Bellamy set sail, local legend indicates that Maria discovered that she was pregnant. Her infant died soon after she gave birth. As a result of the scandal surrounding her pregnancy, she was briefly jailed, disowned by her family, and forced to leave town.[150]

Upon reaching the coast of Florida, Bellamy and his partner Williams were unable to locate any sunken Spanish vessels, so the aspiring treasure seekers did not attain their dream. Rather than undergo the humiliation of returning home empty-handed, Bellamy and his followers decided to become pirates. In April of 1716, Bellamy, who had joined forces with privateer Henry Jennings, captured the French merchantman *St. Marie* which contained an impressive cargo of Spanish gold. Soon thereafter, he met and was invited to join the crew of the famous pirate, Benjamin Hornigold, whose crewmen included the soon to be notorious Edward Teach.[151] Bellamy prospered under the leadership first of Jennings, then Hornigold, but eventually had a serious policy disagreement with the latter. Hornigold was a British subject and, as such, refused to attack any vessel flying the colors of Great Britain. Bellamy and the majority of the crew believed that any merchantman should be fair game for attack and that no exceptions should be made on the basis of nationality. Therefore, following a formal election, Bellamy replaced Hornigold as the *Mary Anne's* captain. Hornigold and the few members of the crew who remained loyal to him, including Edward Teach, took their share of the *Mary Anne's* booty and departed.[152] Over the next year, Bellamy and his crew prospered, capturing approximately fifty vessels.

During the spring of 1717, "Black Sam" and his partner Williams, with their three-vessel fleet captured the British slaver *Whydah*, which was on the final phase of its three-stage voyage. It had acquired a cargo of slaves, traded them for a cargo of gold and other valuable goods, and was homeward bound.[153] Bellamy made friends with the captain of the *Whydah*; and when Bellamy released him, he made a trade, giving him the *Sultana* from his fleet in exchange for the *Whydah*. He re-equipped the *Whydah* as the new 28-gun flagship of his fleet. In April 1717, Bellamy and his fleet set sail for New England, undoubtedly to see his true love and thrill her with his new, exceedingly wealthy status. His partner, Palgrave Williams, elected to visit his wife in Rhode Island and by doing so saved his own life.[154]

After parting ways, Bellamy and the remainder of his small fleet encountered a severe storm involving both dense fog and 40-foot waves off the coast of Cape Cod. The *Whydah* experienced what was undoubtedly the worst shipwreck in the history of piracy. Many of its 148-man crew were swept overboard, and most of the remainder were either killed as the ship broke apart or froze to death in the water just five hundred feet from shore.[155] Only two of the crew *of the Whydah* survived -- Thomas Davis who was tried and found innocent of piracy, and the other survivor, John Julian, a mixture of native Central American and African descent, who was never tried but sold into slavery.[156] Bellamy's companion ship, the *Mary Anne,* ran aground in the storm. The *Mary Anne's* crew, most of whom were drunk on confiscated Madeira, passed the night safely but were soon arrested, tried and convicted of piracy. Bellamy was killed in the wreckage of the *Whydah*, never to see his beloved Maria again.[157]

Bellamy's partner and friend Palgrave Williams, who escaped capture and whose subsequent fate is somewhat shrouded in mystery, is a very interesting historical footnote. His father was a former attorney general of Rhode Island. His mother could trace her lineage back to King Edward I of England. She was an ancestor of the 41st and 43rd Presidents of the United States, the Bushes, as well. His mother's paternal grandfather was an ancestor of Franklin Delano Roosevelt.[158] Also of historical interest is the fact that the half Central American Indian, half African crewmember, "Julian the Indian", was sold into slavery and likely purchased by John Quincy, grandfather of the strong abolitionist President, John Quincy Adams.[159]

Chapter Ten: Charles Vane, the Unluckiest Pirate of Them All

*L*ike so many others of his ilk, Charles Vane burst onto the pirate scene with little if any documentable evidence concerning his youth. Given his intelligence, arrogance, and even wickedness, knowledge of his formative years could prove to be extremely interesting. His obvious cruelty and total disdain for even his own crewmembers as an adult render his demise, although extremely improbable and unlucky from his perspective, an appropriate and just ending to his career.

As noted above, essentially nothing is known about Charles Vane prior to 1715-1716, when he was reputed to have been a member of Henry Jennings' pirate crew. By 1718 he had his own command.[160]

In that same year, one of his best-known engagements took place off the eastern coast of Florida, where a Spanish treasure galleon had struck a submerged reef and partially sunk. A second Spanish vessel attempting to unload the sinking galleon was soon surrounded by a number of pirate ships including Vane's, which were focused on a similar mission. In the midst of this activity, most of the pirates were driven from the area by the sudden appearance of two Spanish men-of-war. Vane, however, waited patiently until these vessels departed on another mission, captured the rescue vessel, seized its treasure, and returned to his home base in New Providence, Bahamas.[161]

While Vane and his crew were pursuing their fortunes at sea, the English monarch had appointed a new Royal Governor in New Providence, Woodes Rogers, whose sole and extremely challenging mission was to rid the area of its unsavory pirate inhabitants. Rogers began his new career by establishing a policy commonly employed throughout the Golden Era. He offered a royal pardon to anyone who would renounce his pirating ways. While many of New Providence's more undesirable occupants were quick to take advantage of the Governor's offer, Vane, after careful thought, sent the following letter to the Governor instead:[162]

To His Excellency The Governor of New Providence

Your Excellency may please to understand that we are willing to accept His Majesty's most gracious pardon on the following terms, viz. That you will suffer us to dispose of all our goods now in our possession. Likewise, to act as we see fit with everything belonging to us, as His Majesty's Act of Grace specifies. If your Excellency shall please to comply with this we shall with all readiness accept of His Majesty's Act of Grace. If not, we are obliged to stand on our defense.

So conclude
Your humble servants

Charles Vane and company

Not surprisingly, Governor Rogers was incensed by Vane's response to his generous offer of a pardon. Determined to make an example of Vane, Rogers sent his flagship to capture him and his crew before they could escape from New Providence. While attempting to escape, Vane set one of his captured vessels on fire and had it sailed directly toward Rogers' flagship, *HMS Rose*.[163] As the flagship turned to maneuver out of the path of the burning vessel, Vane and his men sailed around their would-be captors and fled with their treasure intact. It is reported that as they sailed past the flagship, the pirates jeered at and fired on its crew. Thus, while Charles Vane failed to secure a royal pardon, he definitely earned the reputation as a cunning and skillful pirate captain.

Vane soon established a new base of operations in the Carolinas, where he met another famous Carolina pirate, Edward Teach. The story is told that the two pirates and their crews engaged in an infamous week of drunken debauchery and womanizing that became known in local history as the "Ocracoke Orgy".[164]

Given his daring, his obvious seamanship, and his skill in locating and accumulating treasure, one might think that Vane would have been extremely popular with his crew. However, such was not the case. In the first place, he was exceptionally cruel, known for torturing and murdering many of his captives. He also paid scant attention to the "Pirate's Code", often trying to cheat his crew out of their proper share of stolen booty. When Vane wisely decided to disengage from (or avoid attacking, depending on your source) a bigger and more heavily armed French man-of-war that he should never have attacked in the first place, his disgruntled crew inappropriately accused him of behaving in a cowardly fashion. As a result, they voted to replace him as captain with his first mate, Calico Jack Rackham. Vane and about fifteen of his loyal crewmembers were placed in a small boat and abandoned.[165]

It didn't take long for him to get back on his feet, however, and he soon rebuilt his fleet and returned to the "sweet trade",[166] as buccaneering was often called by its practioners. While in the Bay of Honduras, Vane's small fleet was scattered in a deadly hurricane. Vane's flagship was thrown on rocks in the Bay and sank, with only Vane and possibly one other sailor surviving by swimming to a deserted island.[167]

Although it is not clear what happened to Vane's companion, Vane himself lived for several months on turtles and locally obtained water; and it is possible, although not commonly believed, that his sole remaining crewmember survived along with him. Eventually, a merchantman anchored at the island to take on fresh drinking water. Vane was initially pleased to discover that the merchantman's commander was Captain Holford, a former sailing mate who had renounced his pirate ways. Unfortunately, when Vane asked Holford to take him aboard his ship, the latter replied:[168]

> I shan't trust you aboard my ship unless I carry you a Prisoner, for I shall have you caballing with my Men, knock me on the Head, & run away with my Ship a pyrating.

In spite of Vane's assurances that such was not his intention, Holford remained firm in his suspicions and resolve. Therefore, Vane was forced to remain behind on the deserted island when Holford departed.

A few weeks later a second merchantman put into the island to replenish its water supply, and this time its captain, who didn't know Charles Vane, agreed to take him onboard as a crewmember. While at sea with his new ship and crew, a chance event occurred that would render Vane perhaps the unluckiest pirate ever to pursue his craft. His new vessel happened to encounter the merchantman commanded by Captain Holford. Since the two captains were close friends, they agreed to dine together aboard Vane's new captain's ship.[169] During the meal, Captain Holford chanced to glance down into the ship's open hold where several of the crew, including Charles Vane, were hard at work. Holford immediately informed his friend that Vane was actually a notorious pirate. His friend then had Vane arrested and put in irons. He delivered Vane to Port Royal where he was tried, convicted of piracy, and on March 29, 1720, hanged at Gallows Point, which was, ironically, the same site where "Calico Jack" Rackham, Vane's former quartermaster, would eventually meet his fate.[170] (See Chapter Four for additional information on Vane and the controversy surrounding his personalized Jolly Roger.)

Chapter Eleven: Benjamin Hornigold, the Pirate Tutor

$\mathcal{L}$ ittle is known about the early career of Benjamin Hornigold prior to the War of Spanish Succession. He undoubtedly served as an English privateer during the War; and he also appears to have been a typical example of the seamen who were unemployed at the War's conclusion and reluctantly turned to piracy as a necessary means of support. [171]

While Stede Bonnet may be known as the "Gentleman Pirate" because of his affluent background and education, Hornigold was clearly one of the nicest pirates of the Golden Era. [172] A number of stories are told of his gentlemanly behavior. [173] One such tale evolved from a time when Hornigold and his crew were pursuing a fleeing schooner, which they eventually overtook, captured, and boarded. Hornigold is said to have addressed the ship's captain personally and requested that his crew all surrender their hats. He then rather sheepishly admitted that his own crew had participated in a drunken revelry the preceding night and thrown their hats overboard during the celebration. Taking nothing else of value, Hornigold and his men returned to their own ship, hats in hand, and departed.

He was certainly an able pirate captain, but is better known for the tutelage of some of his more illustrious crewmembers, including Samuel "Black Sam" Bellamy and the soon to be infamous Edward Teach. In fact, he and Teach formed a strong friendship, and it was Hornigold who impressed upon the future Blackbeard the importance of maintaining a perpetually fearsome appearance and reputation. [174]

Hornigold started his pirate career earlier than many suspect, as early as August of 1713 following the end of the War. He and a partner are often credited with initiating piracy in the Bahamas and with declaring New Providence a Pirates' Republic. Depending on your source, his partner was either fellow pirate Thomas Barrow, or old friend John Cochram, [175,176] who ran the business end of a complex smuggling operation. Hornigold, with a crew of over two hundred, took care of business on the sea.

Hornigold's adamant refusal to attack any merchantman flying the British ensign would ultimately prove to be self-destructive and the undoing of his career as a pirate captain. Much of his crew had harbored resentment against this ban, holding the opinion that merchant ships of all nations should be subject to pirate conquest. Eventually, Black Sam Bellamy was able to persuade a majority of the crew to turn against their captain and vote him out of office, replacing him with Black Sam himself. Transfer of command was unusually amicable with Hornigold and his remaining loyal crew, including Edward Teach. They were put adrift in a small boat after receiving their shares of the pirate vessel's captured treasure or booty.[177]

It was at this juncture that Teach and Hornigold parted company. Hornigold elected to return to New Providence while Blackbeard set sail for America and Bath, North Carolina, the state's first town and seaport. Upon returning to the Bahamas, Hornigold was the head of an official welcoming committee of local pirates organized to greet the new Governor, Woodes Rogers, upon his arrival. Governor Rogers, as previously mentioned, offered a one-time royal pardon to all pirates who were willing to renounce their former careers, which Hornigold accepted. Woodes Rogers went one step further and specifically recruited Hornigold as a privateer to assist him in hunting pirates. Once again, Hornigold enthusiastically accepted .[178]

Hornigold's initial targets were Charles Vane, Calico Jack Rackham, and John Auger. Hornigold pursued Vane and Rackman as far as Long Island Sound, but they eventually eluded him.[179] He did succeed in apprehending John Auger and a number of minor pirates, who were subsequently executed. Many feel that the execution of these pirates essentially marked the end of pirating in the Bahamas.

In 1719 Hornigold was on a trading mission to Mexico when his ship disappeared. Most writers feel that he struck a submerged reef and he and all of his crew were drowned. Others suggest that he was captured by the Spanish and thrown into jail for the remainder of his life.[180]

Chapter Twelve: Edward Teach (Blackbeard), The "Fury from Hell"

$\mathcal{I}$n spite of his worldwide fame, the early years of Edward Teach, the infamous Blackbeard, are shrouded in obscurity like those of most of his contemporaries. In fact, only the last 18 months of his life can be accurately documented, according to Sandra MacLean Clunies and Bruce Roberts.[181] His last name has been spelled in a variety of ways, including Teach, Thatch, Thach, Thache, and even Drummond. Similarly, his birthplace has been attributed to Jamaica, Philadelphia, London and Bristol, England, with the latter being the most commonly accepted by historians.

In any event, he likely served as a privateer at some point during Queen Anne's War, the training ground for so many infamous pirates, and by 1716 had joined the crew of Captain Benjamin Hornigold. He captured a French slaver, *La Concorde,* the following year. He renamed the slaver *Queen Anne's Revenge,* outfitted her with forty cannons, and made her the flagship of his small fleet. While Hornigold had accepted a King's pardon during the latter part of that same year and retired, Blackbeard continued on in the sweet trade. Despite being on his own, he never forgot his mentor's most important lesson: always maintain a bold and terrifying image and reputation.[182]

In keeping with this mantra, Teach grew a massive black beard that covered most of his face -- a beard that he braided and tied with black or red ribbons. This striking beard was the obvious source of his famous nickname. He wore a crimson coat and various bandoleers into which were thrust an assortment of pistols and daggers. From under his hat emerged a number of slow-burning fuses that he lit and used during battle, thereby creating a demonic halo of smoke and sparks around his head.[183] Given his imposing frame and his contrived appearance, he certainly projected a "terrifying image" for all those who first set eyes upon him.

His deeds often matched his appearance. For example, Terrance Zepke[184] tells the following story:

> Once when the pirate leader, his trusted first mate, and another crew member were seated around a table in Teach's cabin drinking and socializing, Blackbeard quietly pulled a pistol from one of his numerous shoulder and waist gun slings and shot his first mate, Israel Hands, in the kneecap. As the crippled-for-life man screamed in agony, he managed to cry out "Why?" to which Blackbeard laughingly bellowed, "If I don't kill somebody now and then, you'll forget who I am!"

Nevertheless, the ladies loved him, and he enthusiastically returned that love. Legend has it that he "married" at least 13 times during his brief career.[185] Rather than avail himself of the numerous prostitutes in the various ports he frequented, he would supposedly go ashore and find an attractive young girl who appealed to him. He would return with her to his vessel and have one of his crew "marry" them. The marriage would usually endure until the *Queen Anne's Revenge* and her sister ships sailed from the port in question.

The appointment of a new Royal Governor in Jamaica foretold the beginning of the end of the colony as a safe haven for pirates, and Blackbeard recognized the need to find a new base of operations.[186] In January of 1718, he set sail for the coast of North Carolina, eventually establishing his headquarters in Carolina's first settlement and seaport, Bath Town.[187]   Charles Eden, Governor of North Carolina at that time, was supposed to be favorably disposed to pirates whom he may have regarded as a source of increased maritime trade for the State; i.e., pirates sold their hard to acquire contraband to local merchants, often at significantly discounted prices. Rumors abound that he was a close friend and may have even been a business partner of Edward Teach. Terrance Zepke[188] notes that "...according to local legend, a tunnel that ran from Bath Town Creek to the basement of Governor Eden's house was used for the purpose of smuggling stolen goods."

While Blackbeard is reputed to have captured and looted over 50 ships in his career, his most daring feat occurred in May of 1718 when he blockaded the city of Charleston, South Carolina. His ships remained offshore at the mouth of Charleston harbor, and soon captured eight merchantmen, seizing some of Charleston's most prominent citizens as their prisoners. Among those held captive was Samuel Wragg, a member of the South Carolina Council of State.   Blackbeard sent one of these prisoners with two of his own crew to meet with Governor Johnson.   As instructed by Blackbeard, the crewmen demanded a ransom that included a large chest of medicines for the release of the Charleston captives. They noted that their prisoners' lives would be forfeit if Blackbeard's demands were not speedily and completely met.[189] Some think that Blackbeard was contemplating retiring from piracy, and that the looting of the Charleston ships and the ransom for their passengers was to construct his own "golden parachute" for his retirement years.   Others suggest that Blackbeard may have contracted a venereal disease from one of his many wives, and that the medicine chest was to be put to more personal and immediate use.

Once he received his ransom, he released his captives and set sail for North Carolina. Upon reaching the Carolina coast, he sailed his small flotilla into Topsail Inlet where he either deliberately or accidentally ran his flagship and the sloop *Adventure* aground on a sandbar. Many feel that Blackbeard, foreseeing the end of his days as a pirate, deliberately wanted to reduce the size of his fleet and his crew, which had reached four ships and over 400 seamen.[190] A smaller fleet would be harder to track, and a smaller crew would certainly reduce the number of shares into which his hoard of "ill-gotten treasure" would need to be divided.[191] He marooned some of his crew on a sandbar, and abandoned others, including his "partner" Stede Bonnet, whom he had supposedly sent inland to acquire supplies. As a result of these villainous activities, Teach reduced his flotilla to a single sloop, *Adventure* (smaller than the one that had been grounded with the *Queen Anne's Revenge*), with a crew of 40 whites and 60 blacks. It has even been suggested that Blackbeard may have intended to sell the blacks back into slavery or trade them, which would certainly have been in keeping with his character.[192]

When he returned to Bath, he applied for and was granted a pardon from Governor Eden for his previous acts of piracy, including the blockade of Charleston. It is rumored that the Governor even presided at Teach's wedding to a sixteen-year-old planter's daughter, Mary Ormond, who finally agreed to marry him once he renounced his life of piracy. She apparently was his one true love, and he was willing to agree to anything to make her his bride.[193]

There is a local folk tale, which may or may not be true, that Mary was seriously involved with another man and originally would have nothing to do with Teach. According to this story, it is said that one day she received a package containing the would-be suitor's ring finger and signet ring along with a note indicating that this finger was all she would ever see of him again.

After a short interlude of marital bliss Blackbeard's restless spirit predictably drove him back to the only life he really knew, that of a pirate. He set sail in his sole surviving ship for Bermuda and promptly seized two French merchant ships loaded with valuable cargo. He placed all of the cargo in one of the ships, released the French crewmembers to the other, and returned to North Carolina. In Bath he informed Governor Eden that he had found the French merchantman "abandoned" on the high seas. Once again, he added to his collection of pardons from Governor Eden.[194]

While the North Carolina Governor appeared to believe or, at least, officially accept his tale, others were not as understanding. Governor Alexander Spotswood of Virginia, strongly opposed to piracy and involved in a bitter campaign for re-election, declared Blackbeard's Charleston Harbor blockade pardon from Governor Eden to be null and void because of his latest transgression. Although Spotswood was clearly in violation of the royal "Act of Grace" upon which Blackbeard's pardon was based, he proceeded to acquire two appropriate naval ships and crew them with British seamen in order to pursue the "Terror from Hell" with the hope of bringing his career to an end.[195] The commander of this pursuit was a Lieutenant Maynard, the oldest lieutenant in the British navy, who desperately needed an important victory in order to propel his stagnant career forward.[196] Thus, both primary individuals involved in the pursuit would seem to have had a strong personal interest in Blackbeard's apprehension.

The two British sloops sailed to Ocracoke Inlet in November; and at dawn on the twenty-second of the month; the battle between pirates and British seamen ensued. Clunies and Roberts[197] note, "Tradition has it that Blackbeard's first cannon volley killed more than twenty men, including Captain Hyde, and crippled Hyde's ship, the *Ranger*." On board the surviving British sloop *Jane*, Maynard had most of his crew hide below deck, thereby tricking Blackbeard into believing that he had vanquished his pursuers. When Blackbeard and his fellow pirates boarded their presumed "prize", they were met by Maynard and his crew and an intense hand-to-hand combat broke out. As Blackbeard and Maynard were locked in a bitter struggle, another British seaman struck Blackbeard with a vicious blow to the neck, nearly severing his head from his body. However, according to Terrance Zepke, the pirate chief didn't die until he had been shot five times and received over twenty cutlass wounds.[198] Maynard completed the task of severing Blackbeard's head from his body, and then threw the body overboard.[199] Local legend claims that Blackbeard's body swam out around the *Jane* three times in search of its head, but to no avail.[200] The head was returned to Governor Spotswood in Virginia as proof of the successful completion of the mission.[201]

Blackbeard played a critical role in a discussion that I had with a seven-year-old boy, decked out in a do rag, eye patch, and toothbrush-style mustache at a recent Baldhead Island, NC, pirate festival. At the conclusion of my presentation, he asked me what I considered a pirate's favorite weapon to be. I assured him that I knew he was familiar with the most common weapons employed by pirates such as the blunderbuss, pistol, sword, cutlass, dagger, grenade, belaying pin, and boarding hook. I also asked if he was aware that pirates often soaped or greased the deck of their ships in order to make them slippery and help repel potential boarders. Or, that they scattered large, sharp tacks across the decks to injure these same, often-barefooted potential boarders? When he replied that he didn't, I told him that it really didn't matter since none of them was a pirate's favorite weapon in my opinion. Instead, I believe that any pirate worth his salt relied on fear as his most effective weapon. I used Blackbeard as my model of an infamous pirate who relied heavily on fear. And, as discussed in Chapter Four, I also noted that many of the more notorious pirates in history are reputed to have employed this same weapon of fear in the form of a personalized Jolly Roger to inform their intended victims of exactly whom they were facing. Hopefully, these victims would be so terrified that they would surrender without a shot being fired.

Finally, as a partial defense of Teach, I noted that his many wives, his potential willingness to sell his black crew members into slavery, his shooting of his first mate and best friend in the knee as a jest, and countless other tales clearly attest to his lack of character or conscience. But, in the end, he may have been a real mixture of both flamboyance and evil rather than pure evil alone. For example, there are some historians who feel that he may never have killed an opponent in battle, which would seem to argue against evil being the sole aspect if his personality.

Chapter Thirteen: Stede Bonnet, the Gentleman Pirate

tede Bonnet, the Gentleman Pirate, is one of the more interesting buccaneers in the history of the Carolinas during the Golden Age. He was certainly one of the highest ranking socially and the most educated. He also was one of the least likely and least qualified men ever to pursue the pirate trade on the high seas.

According to Clunies and Roberts,[202] Stede Bonnet was baptized at Christ Church in Barbados on July 29, 1688. Both of his parents died in 1694, so Stede and his two younger sisters were orphaned at an early age. The death of his legal guardian soon after that of his parents undoubtedly contributed further to what was in all likelihood an unhappy childhood. On September 21, 1709, Stede married Mary Allamby, the daughter of a wealthy planter, and significantly enhanced his financial standing.[203] Bonnet served in the colonial militia during Queen Anne's War with France, attaining the rank of Major. Before his 30th birthday he completed his service and retired to the family's sugar plantation in Barbados. There, in Bridgetown, he pursued a life of social prominence and leisure. Suddenly, probably sometime in 1717, to the utter astonishment of his friends and neighbors, he renounced plantation life, purchased a sloop, and launched his new career as a pirate.[204]

A number of explanations have been advanced for Bonnet's abrupt and dramatic change in lifestyle. Some feel that as a former active military man, he had become bored with the unexciting routine of plantation living, much like his fellow pirates William Kidd and Edward Teach. Given his pronounced love of books and reading, however, this explanation seems unlikely. Many asserted that he had fallen victim to a sudden mental breakdown. Others felt he was escaping his nagging shrew of a wife. Finally, some combined the last two theories to conclude that his wife's perpetual nagging had brought about a mental breakdown.

In any event, he immediately achieved a unique position in the annals of piracy by buying his sloop instead of capturing or stealing it.[205] He equipped his vessel with ten guns, renamed her the *Revenge,* which, according to Zepke, was the most common name for a pirate ship, and hired an experienced quartermaster, Israel Morton. Morton, in turn, heavily recruited within the local taverns and eventually hired a crew of seventy seamen.[206,207] This recruitment process marked yet another first in pirate history, since pirate crewmembers traditionally worked for contractual shares of any captured treasure rather than wages.[208]

Bonnet flew his own personalized Jolly Roger atop the Revenge. His ensign was known as the "Pirate's Scale". It supposedly featured a skull below which a single bone was stretched, with a dagger on one side and a heart on the other, representing the balance between life and death. He completed the equipping of the sloop by bringing his extensive personal library on board ship, again distinguishing himself from the buccaneering norm.[209]

Bonnet and his crew set sail for Virginia and the Carolinas, where they initially succeeded in capturing a number of prizes. As time passed, however, a rapidly expanding gulf developed between the captain and his crew. In addition to the personality peculiarities noted above, Stede Bonnet always dressed in a gentlemanly (some might even say foppish) manner, rarely drank, and suffered from reoccurring bouts of seasickness.[210] Morale was bordering on mutiny when Bonnet met up with his piratical mirror image, the infamous Blackbeard. Teach developed an amused if short-lived liking for Bonnet and a sincere fondness for his sloop the *Revenge*.[211] They immediately entered into some sort of partnership, which may well have prevented Bonnet's death at the hands of his own crew. Blackbeard shrewdly convinced Bonnet that a gentleman of his social prominence should not be involved with the actual sailing of a ship, invited him aboard the *Queen Anne's Revenge*, and replaced him behind the wheel of his sloop with a trusted member of his own crew.[212] Bonnet spent most of his time on Blackbeard's flagship in his dressing gown reading books from his library. Whether he realized it or not, he was virtually Blackbeard's prisoner.

Bonnet was with Blackbeard during the blockade of Charles Town (Charleston, SC), and sailed back with him to North Carolina following the ransom payment and release of the captured Charlestonians. Upon reaching Beaufort Inlet, North Carolina, Blackbeard (as discussed in the preceding chapter) decided to reduce the size of his fleet and crews. After grounding his own flagship and Bonnet's schooner, he sent Bonnet on a diversionary errand, removed everything of value from the *Revenge*, marooned Bonnet's remaining crew on a sandbar, and made off with the undivided ransom.

Following his return from his spurious mission for supplies, Bonnet reclaimed his sloop, rescued his crew from the sandbar, and set off in pursuit of Blackbeard. Fortunately for him, he was unable to apprehend Teach, who would undoubtedly have dispatched him with ease. Bonnet spent the next three months capturing ships off the Delaware Bay–Virginia coastal area. In response to Blackbeard's suggestion, Bonnet had applied for a royal pardon, changed his name to Thomas and the name of the *Revenge* to the *Royal James* in order to protect himself until the application process was completed.[213]

In September of 1718, Bonnet landed in a small cove at the edge of Southport, NC, to effect a number of major repairs to his sloop. (The actual location is directly across Moore Street from the development known as Bonnet's Landing, four blocks from my home.) This decision proved to be his undoing.

Unbeknownst to Bonnet/Thomas, South Carolina Governor Johnson had dispatched Colonel Rhett, 150 seamen, and two sloops, the *Henry* and the *Sea Nymph*, to capture pirates operating in the region and bring them to justice.[214] Many feel that Rhett was seeking more notorious prey, such as Captain Charles Vane, when he and his crew happened upon Bonnet and his men. After failing an attempt to escape, Bonnet surrendered to Rhett on September 27[215] following a fierce, five hour-long struggle, and he and his crew were taken to Charleston for trial.

While his crew was placed under guard, Bonnet, being a gentleman, was afforded more freedom as befitted his social status. As a man of letters, he sent the South Carolina Governor what could well be one of the most self-effacing pleas for mercy ever penned:[216]

Honoured Sir;

I Have presumed on the Confidence of your emminent Goodness to throw myself, after this manner at your Feet, to implore you'll be graciously pleased to look upon me with tender Bowels of Pity and Compassion; and believe me to be the most miserable Man this Day breathing; That the Tears proceeding from my most sorrowful Soul may soften your Heart, and incline you to consider my Dismal State, wholly, I must confess, unprepared to receive so soon the dreadful Execution you have been pleased to appoint me; and therefore beseech you to think me an Object of your Mercy.

For God's Sake, good Sir, let the Oaths of three Christian Men weigh something with you, who are ready to depose, when you please to allow them the Liberty, the Compulsion I lay under in committing those Acts for which I am doomed to die.

I intreat you not to let me fall a Sacrifice to the Envy and ungodly Rage of some few Men, who, not being yet satisfied with Blood, feign to believe that I had the Happiness of a longer Life in this World, I should still employ it in a wicked Manner, which to remove that, and all other Doubts with your Honour, I heartily beseech you'll permit me to live, and I'll voluntarily put it ever out of my Power by separating all my Limbs from my Body, only reserving the use of my Tongue to call continually on, and pray to the Lord, my God, and mourn all my Days in Sackcloth and Ashes to work out confident Hopes of my Salvation, at that great and dreadful Day when all righteous Souls shall receive their just rewards: And to render your

Honour a further Assurance of my being incapable to prejudice any of
my Fellow-Christians, if I was so wickedly bent, I humbly beg you
will, (as a Punishment of my Sins for my poor Soul's Sake) indent me
as a menial Servant to your Honour and this Government during my
Life, and send me up to the farthest inland Garrison or settlement in
the Country, or in any other ways you'll be pleased to dispose of me;
and likewise that you'll receive the Willingness of my Friends to be
bound for my good Behavior and Constant attendance to your
Commands.
I once more beg for the Lord's Sake, dear Sir, that as you are a
Christian, you will be as Charitable as to have Mercy and
Compassion on my miserable Soul, but too newly awaked from an
Habit of Sin to entertain so Confident Hopes and Assurances of its
being received into the arms of Blessed Jesus, as is necessary to
reconcile me to so speedly a Death; wherefore as my Life, Blood,
Reputation of my family and future happy State lies entirely at your
Disposal, I implore you to consider me with a Christian and
Charitable Heart, and determine mercifully of me that I may ever
acknowledge and esteem you next to God, my Saviour, and oblige me
ever to pray that our heavenly Father will also forgive your
Trespasses.
Now the God of Peace, that brought again from the Dead our Lord
Jesus, that great Sheperd of the Sheep thru' the Blood of the
everlasting Covenant, make you Perfect in every good work to do his
Will, working in you that which is well pleasing in his Sight through
Jesus Christ, to whom be Glory forever and ever, is the hearty Prayer
of

Your Honour's
Most miserable &,
Afflicted Servent
Stede Bonnet

Bonnet was nonetheless unwilling to rely merely on the common belief
that he would be shown mercy because of his former social position and
background, or on his own written pleadings. Therefore, he disguised himself
as a woman and escaped with his sailing master, David Herriot.[217] The two
fugitives stole a small boat, and fled from Charleston. The incensed Governor
ordered Colonel Rhett to pursue the escapees and return them to face justice.
After twelve days Rhett did capture the two pirates, killing Herriot in the
process. Bonnet was tried, condemned to death with no merciful intervention
from the Governor, and hung a month after the execution of his crew on
December 10, 1715. Interestingly, his execution occurred within two to three
week's of Blackbeard's decapitation.[218] Sobbing as he marched to meet his
executioner, he had to be supported by two guards to keep him from fainting.

Between his shackled hands was a small wilted nosegay symbolically reflecting his sorrow for his sins. Including the twenty-nine crewmembers who had been hung the previous month, his death marked the largest mass execution that had ever taken place in this country.[219] Bonnet's body was allowed to remain hanging from the gallows for four days as a warning to any who might contemplate following in his footsteps. It is reported that Colonel Rhett strongly disliked Governor Johnson for hanging Bonnet since Rhett had given his word to the pirate that he wouldn't be executed if he surrendered.[220]

The hanging of
Stede Bonnett

Since Stede Bonnet is by far my favorite pirate, I cannot conclude this tale without explaining why that is so. He was well educated, and so am I. In fact, my father, my long suffering wife, and her parents would all have agreed that I was overeducated, even before I seriously contemplated going to medical school after finally receiving my Ph.D.

There is also the issue of what prompted Bonnet to renounce his comfortable lifestyle and become a pirate. While we cannot say with absolute certainty that it was due to his wife's nagging, it appears to be a very plausible explanation. One of my wife's first Valentines to me was a framed, cross-stitched sampler that proclaimed "A Nagging Wife May Save Your Life". It hung over my desk throughout my working career.

As I noted in the Foreword, we retired to the North Carolina coast, just four blocks from the site where Bonnet and his crew were accidentally apprehended. I, like Bonnet before me, feel that I might be the only male living at the coast who has no interest in or knowledge of boats and sailing. I love sea breezes as they blow across the land, but that is about as close to being a sailor, as I will ever come.

Furthermore, I am not much of a drinker or gambler, love to read, and would probably stay in my pajamas or dressing gown all day if the community college where I teach remedial math would allow it.

Finally, I would like to think that with nearly one thousand years of the Irish tradition of embracing combat, particularly with the British, behind me, I would have fearlessly mounted the gallows' steps to face my executioner. However, out of the corner of my mind's eye, I am afraid that I can see two pairs of hands, each supporting one of my elbows, to keep me from fainting. I guess that while I consider Bonnet to be the most inept pirate to ever sail the seas, I know that he is the Golden Age pirate I would be most likely to emulate.

Chapter Fourteen: Edward "Ned" Low,
Avery's Main Rival for the "Most Despicable Pirate"

ome historians regard Henry "Long Ben" Avery as the most despicable pirate ever to set sail. Others assert that this characterization could just as readily be applied to another but less well-known buccaneer, Edward "Ned" Low. Anthony E. Bakker, author of *Charleston & The Golden Age of Piracy,*[221] asserts that he was a "psychopathic sadist whose cruelties knew no bounds" and "the lowest of all that sailed the seas during the Golden Age of Piracy". Harsh words indeed!

In any event, Edward Low was born around 1690 in Westminster, London, to a family with strong inclinations toward petty criminality. Not surprisingly, he was well acquainted with poverty and certainly uneducated from an academic perspective. On the other hand Low aggressively launched his professional career at a very early age. He appears to have begun as a petty thief and gambler, graduated to membership in a pickpocket gang that may have included his older brother, and culminated his childhood crime spree by breaking into houses.[222] Eventually, he must have realized that his opportunities were rapidly disappearing while the chances of his being apprehended were dramatically increasing. So, he took to life on the sea, again, possibly, accompanied by his older brother. They supposedly devoted a few years to developing their skills as sailors, then decided to settle in Boston, Massachuetts.[223]

Surprisingly, Edward Low spent some time legitimately employed as a ship rigger while living in Boston.[224] But his frequently uncontrollable temper eventually surfaced, and he had a serious falling out with his employer, leading to his dismissal. During this time period, he apparently fell deeply in love for the first and only time in his life, marrying Eliza Marble.[225] His wife bore him a son, who died in infancy, and then a daughter, Elizabeth. Unfortunately, Eliza died during the birth of their daughter, which was not at all uncommon in that era.[226] Low was presumably so grief stricken over the loss of his wife that he reverted to his earlier upbringing, ultimately turning to a life of piracy and, essentially, abandoning his daughter in Boston.[227]

By 1722, Low had joined the crew of a sloop planning on sailing to Honduras, stealing a cargo of logwood, and returning to Boston with the logwood in order to resell it. He soon formed a strong bond with twelve of the least reputable members of the crew. One day during this journey, Low and his companions had a serious falling out with their captain; and, as several authors have suggested, attempted to mutiny and shoot their captain. Their soon-to-be ex-captain thwarted their violent efforts, and the rebellious seamen were forced overboard in the ship's longboat. By the next day, Low and his companions had stolen a small vessel off the coast of Rhode Island and dramatically launched their new careers as pirates.[228]

Beginning around May of 1722, Low assembled a small fleet of 3-4 ships from vessels that he had captured, greatly enhancing his reputation for both piracy and cruelty. His various bases of operation included the coast of New England, the Azores, and the Caribbean. During this period, he met and occasionally joined forces with other infamous pirates such as Captain George Lowther. Yet he will undoubtedly be better remembered for his barbaric behavior than his buccaneering conquests. His extremely cruel method of torturing victims in order to extract information serves as an illustrative example of this behavior. He would light a match or rope fuse between victims' fingers, and let it burn their skin down to the bone unless they revealed what he wanted to know.[229] Possibly his most disgusting act of cruelty is rumored to have been used as a punishment for those victims who angered him (e.g., by attempting to conceal money from him), He would cut off the victim's lips, have them boiled and salted, and make the victim eat them before he dispatched him.[230] Low's cruelty was not limited to obtaining information forcibly or meting out punishment; he was known to behave in this barbaric manner for his own personal amusement as well.[231] During his plundering of the Azores, Madeira, and the Canary Islands, he offered the Governor the opportunity to free prisoners from seven vessels he had captured around St. John's by trading Low badly needed fresh water and supplies. When fulfilling his part of the bargain, Low retained a captured French cook, noting that he was a "greasy fellow" who would fry well. Low then proceeded to prove his point while the victim was still alive.[232] Yet, he is supposed to have continued to grieve over the death of his wife and the abandonment of his daughter to such an extent that he always returned female captives to shore unharmed.[233]

Low spent much of 1763 plying his trade and increasing his outrageous reputation first in Newfoundland and then the Azores. He teamed up with an old friend, Captain Charles Harris, and eventually headed to Charleston, South Carolina. North of Charleston, they encountered a British man-of-war, *HMS Greyhound*, and a ferocious and prolonged battle ensued. After several hours of fighting, Low decided to abandon his friend, leaving him at the mercy of Captain Peter Solgard and the *Greyhound*. He succeeded in escaping at his friend's expense. Harris and his entire crew were soon captured, and 25 pirates were hanged at Newport, Rhode Island, on July 19, 1723.[234] Captain Harris was sent back to Wrapping, England, where he received a similar trial and fate.

There are conflicting stories about how Low finally met his end, although it is likely to have occurred sometime in the next year. "The Pirate's Realm" presents two likely tales of how Low may have met his demise.[235] The first version claims that after his escape from Charleston, Low was seen sailing in the Canary Islands where he is assumed to have been lost at sea during a storm. A second, and possibly more compelling version, given his character, claims that he had a violent argument with his quartermaster and murdered him that night while he lay sleeping. Low's crew then rebelled and put him adrift in a small boat with two of his followers. Eventually, a ship from Martinique picked up their boat. Once Low was recognized, he was secured and presented to the proper authorities on the Island, where he was tried, found guilty of piracy and murder, and hanged. There are even a small number of writers who support the theory that he escaped unharmed and lived out the remainder of his life as a free man.

While Edward "Ned" Low and Henry "Long Ben" Avery bore similar villainous reputations, there was a marked difference between them. Avery was the arch type red Jolly Roger pirate. Once he gave warning not to resist his takeover of your vessel, failure to heed his demand would result in death for all captives. Furthermore, he appeared not to feel the slightest remorse for his actions, essentially regarding them as normal or appropriate behavior. It seems that Low, on the other hand, sincerely enjoyed cruelty for its own sake. His ensign or personalized Jolly Roger was reputedly a bold red skeleton on a black field. The colors could easily have been reversed with no increase in threat to viewers and potential captives. Taken together, these two pirates clearly dispel the movie-invented image of a buccaneer as a gallant swashbuckler, often worthy of our admiration.

Chapter Fifteen: Bartholomew "Black Bart" Roberts, Last Great Pirate of the Golden Age

A number of authorities such as Captain John Roberts feel that Bartholomew Roberts may well have been the greatest pirate of the Golden Age, far surpassing such better-known rivals as Blackbeard and William Kidd. In his brief thirty-month career (1718–1722) it has been estimated that he captured between 400 and 500 ships.[236]

Bartholomew, a Welshman, was born in the latter part of the seventeenth century as John Roberts, but subsequently changed his first name to Bartholomew. By 1719 he was serving as the third mate on a slaver owned by the Royal Africa Company.[237]

Roberts' slave ship was captured in 1719 by two pirate vessels, the Royal Review and a companion vessel commanded by Captain Howell Davis, a fellow Welshman.[238] Roberts was given an opportunity to join the pirate crew; and while initially reluctant, he soon embraced his new life-style. According to his unofficial biographer, Captain John Roberts, Bartholomew is reputed to have said:[239]

> In an honest service there is thin commons, low wages, and hard labor. In this [occupation of piracy], plenty and satiety, pleasure and ease, liberty and power; and who would not balance creditor on this side, when all the hazard that is run for it, at worst is only a sour look or two at choking? No, a merry life and a short one shall be my motto.

Davis took a quick liking to Roberts, because of both his navigational skills as well as their shared heritage, which allowed them to speak freely to each other in a tongue that few understood.

In the fall of 1719, the *Royal Review,* masquerading as anti-pirate privateer, sailed into the harbor of the Isle of Principe. Captain Davis invited the Portuguese Governor to lunch, planning to hold him for ransom. However, the Portuguese, knowing of Davis' reputation (or having been informed of his plans) arranged for an ambush prior to the lunch — an ambush in which Davis was killed. Back on board the *Royal Review,* the crew elected Bartholomew Roberts to replace their assassinated captain, even though he had only been a member of the ship's company for six weeks. In his acceptance speech Black Bart reportedly noted[240] that he:

…had dipped his Hands in Muddy Water, and must be a Pyrate, [so] it was better being a Commander than a common Man.

As the *Royal Review's* new Captain, Roberts's first official act was to bombard the fort and port (or, again depending on your source, to attack the Port of Principe, kill most of its male inhabitants, and carry off anything of value that could be found by his crew). In any event, Roberts made it quite clear that anyone who confronted him did so at great risk.

During the next two and one-half years, Roberts and his followers rewrote the history of piracy, terrorizing the northeastern coast of the British colonies in America, the Caribbean, and the West African coast as well. In the initial phase of his campaign, he flew his first personalized Jolly Roger that supposedly depicted Roberts and the Devil jointly holding an hourglass.[241]

During this same period, the buccaneers observed a brigantine, and Roberts and forty of his men pursued her in a small sloop, which they had captured. While Roberts and his men were engaged in their pursuit, Walter Kennedy, whom Roberts had left in charge of his mother ship, *the Rover*, and a treasure hoard of approximately 30,000 pounds in gold coins, appear to have deserted Roberts. Undaunted, he renamed his remaining sloop the *Fortune*, and drew up the following set of articles to which the entire crew swore their allegiance:[242]

I. Every man has a vote in affairs of moment; but equal title to the fresh provisions or strong liquors at any time seized, and use them at pleasure unless a scarcity make it necessary for the good of all to vote a retrenchment….

II. Every man to be called fairly in turn, by list, on board of prizes, because over and above a proper share is allowed a shift of clothes. But if a crew member defrauds the Company to the value of a dollar, in plate, jewels, or money, punishment is by marooning. … If the robbery is between one another, the two will content themselves with slitting the ears and nose of him that is guilty, and set him on shore, not in an uninhabited place, but somewhere where he is sure to encounter hardships…

III. No person to game at cards or dice for money…

IV. The lights and candles to be put out at eight o'clock at night; if any of the crew after that hour still remain for drinking, it must be done on the open deck...

V. Must keep all pistols and cutlass clean and fit for service...

VI. No boy or woman allowed amongst crew. Any man found seducing any of the latter sex and carrying her to sea in disguise will suffer death...

VII. To desert the ship or quarters in battle is punished by death or marooning...

VIII. No striking one another on Board, but every man's quarrels will be ended on shore by sword and pistol...

IX. No man to talk of breaking up their way of living till each has shared 1,000 pieces of eight...

X. The Captain and the Quartermaster to receive two shares of a prize, the Master, Boatswain and Gunner one share and a half, and other officers one and one quarter...

XI. The musicians to rest on Sabbath Day, but the other six days and nights, none without special favor...

Robert's also adopted a new personalized flag, depicting him standing astride two heads presumably representing a Barbadian and a Martiniquan. Soon, he is said to have modified his flag once again, depicting himself standing on two skulls -- one labeled ABH for a Barbadian skull and the other AMH for a Martiniquan skull.

As a result of Roberts and his fellow buccaneers' activities during the latter portion of Roberts' career, there was a pronounced lack of seaborne merchant activity in the West Indies. Therefore, Roberts in the *Royal Fortune* and Thomas Anstis in charge of Robert's sister-ship, the *Good Fortune,* next set sail for West Africa.[243] Anstis decided to return to the West Indies at some point in their voyage, while Roberts proceeded on to West Africa. "Black Bart" and his crew were anchored off shore from Cape Lopez on February 10, 1722, when they were challenged by the *H.M.S. Swallow* under Captain Challoner Ogle.[244] When the *Royal Fortune* attempted to sail around the *Swallow*, the British ship fired a grapeshot broadside into her, hitting Roberts in the neck and instantly killing him. The crew threw his body overboard so that it would not be captured by the British, and continued the heated battle for two to three hours.[245]

  After the leaderless crew surrendered, they were taken to Cape Coast Castle, where they were tried, convicted, and executed in one of the largest mass hangings yet to occur. Many historians feel that Roberts' death essentially marks the end of the Golden Period of Piracy.

Chapter Sixteen: John "Calico Jack" Rackham, One of the Most Over-rated Pirates of the Golden Age

Illustration by Kyle Dixon

*J*t is interesting that if we proceed on a chronological basis, the tale of "Black Bart" Roberts, perhaps the most successful pirate of the Golden Age, is immediately followed by the story of "Calico Jack" Rackham, one of the least successful and most over-rated buccaneers of the period. "Calico Jack", so-called because of his foppish manner of dressing in often brightly colored calico, was probably better known in the annals of piracy for being captain of two of the most infamous petticoat pirates of the Golden Age than he was for any individual achievement of his own. His personal focus tended to be on fishing boats and small costal trading ships; and it is very likely that we still remember his name today primarily because of much more notorious female crewmembers.[246-248]

As is often the case, little is known about his early history. What we do know is that by 1718 he was the quartermaster aboard the widely feared pirate ship, the *William,* captained by the much better known and clearly more infamous Charles Vane. In November, the *William* attacked what Vane assumed was a large French merchantman, only to discover that the intended victim was actually a French man-of-war. (See Chapter Ten.) After the man-of-war greeted the *William*'s attack with a thunderous broadside, Vane decided that discretion was the better part of valor and disengaged. Once they were safely away, the crew turned on their unpopular captain, deposed him for what they inappropriately regarded as cowardly behavior, and replaced him with Calico Jack Rackham, not necessarily the best of choices.

By May of 1719, Rackham had lost his ship and returned to New Providence to accept a pardon; in return for this "Act of Grace" he would renounce piracy forever. While in New Providence, he met and fell in love with the beautiful Anne Bonny. Anne had grown tired of her husband-of-convenience, James Bonny, and eventually returned Rackham's affections.

When Rackham tried to bribe her husband to grant her a divorce, Bonny instead appealed to the Governor to have his wife publicly flogged for adultery -- a one-sided punishment that applied only to the female involved in an affair. The Governor upheld his request and set a date for the punishment to be administered. The night before Anne's anticipated public whipping, Rackham assembled a small crew of eight that included Anne dressed as a man. The crew boldly stole the sloop *William,* and returned to sea and the sweet trade.[249]

For the next several months Rackham and his crew patrolled the waters off the coast of Cuba and succeeded in capturing a number of small ships. One of their captures was a Dutch merchantman whose crew included a skilled English seaman and fighter who was soon persuaded to join Rackman and his fellow pirates. Anne Bonny immediately took a strong liking to this new crewmember -- so much so that Calico Jack was beset with jealously. In a fit of rage he threatened to kill the new sailor for Anne's presumed infidelity, only to have Anne introduce him to her newest friend, Mary Read.[250]

Terrance Zepke speculates, "Rackham was so relieved that Anne was not having an affair that he didn't even care that he had been outwitted. "He may have cared more if the entire story had been told -- that Anne had originally been interested in starting an affair with someone."[251]

During this period, Anne is reputed to have become pregnant and was sent by Calico Jack to Cuba to have her baby. He and his crew continued to seize small prizes in the West Indies, and then headed to Bermuda to restock provisions. Once again, their actions brought them to the attention of Governor Woodes Rogers, who took special umbridge at previously pardoned pirates resuming their trade. On September 5, 1720, the Governor issued a proclamation against Rackham and his crew, and sent two naval sloops to apprehend them.[252] Captain Jonathan Barnet, commander of one of the two sloops, came upon Rackham's anchored sloop at Point Negril, the farthest western point of Jamaica. Most of Calico Jack's crew were far too drunk from the previous night's celebration to offer any resistance to the British, and immediately retreated down into their ship's hold when the British attacked. In fact, the only real attempt to repel the British was made by the two petticoat pirates, Anne, who was back onboard the *William,* and Mary. The ladies divided their attention between cursing and fighting the British and swearing and firing into the ship's hold, where their male counterparts were attempting to hide.[253]

The entire crew was eventually captured and taken to the Spanish Town, Jamaica, jail to await trial. On November 16, 1720, Rackham and his ten male crewmembers were tried and found guilty of piracy. They were executed by hanging at Gallows Point and Kingston over the next two days.[254] The fate of their more famous female compatriots is discussed in the section on the petticoat pirates.

Chapter Seventeen: Christopher Condent,
a Ruthless but Successful Pirate

$\mathcal{C}$hristopher Condent would have earned a place in this pirate overview for his striking flag, which featured three skulls and crossed bones side-by-side in a row, alone if nothing else. Yet, his career, while brief, certainly rivals that of many of his better-known contemporaries of the Golden Age in ferocity.

Condent was most likely born in the last decade of the seventeenth century in Plymouth, England.[255] He and his men comprised one of the many pirate crews to flee New Providence in 1718 when Woodes Rogers was first appointed Governor of Bermuda by the English Crown. Subsequently Condent and his crew were sailing across the Atlantic when a crazed East Indian crewman, who had been severely beaten and was seeking revenge, placed their ship in imminent peril. He threatened to ignite the ship's magazine and destroy their vessel. In a display of the daring and resourcefulness for which he was to become famous, Condent jumped into the hold and shot the Indian in the face, thereby saving himself and his crewmates.[256]

The pirates continued their voyage across the Atlantic where they encountered and subsequently captured an English ship. For some reason not fully known, a disagreement broke out among the crew. As a result, half of the crewmen departed on the captured merchantman, while the remainder stayed with their original vessel, electing Condent as their new captain.[257]

Proceeding on to the Cape Verde Islands, Condent and his men captured a fleet of salt ships, a Portuguese wine merchantman, and a Dutch war ship, which surrendered after receiving a single broadside from the pirates. Condent retained the latter for his own use, rechristening it *The Flying Dragon*.[258] *The Flying Dragon* and the remainder of Condent's small fleet then sailed for Brazilian waters, seizing additional booty and occasionally torturing some of their victims by cutting off their noses and/or ears. Next, they journeyed to the African coast and then on to Indian waters where they remained for a year or more. In the fall of 1720, Condent captured an East Indian merchantman, whose cargo constituted a fabulous fortune. The silver and gold alone are reputed to have been worth over 150,000 English pounds, or many millions of dollars by today's standards. Realizing that the East India Company would undoubtedly seek retaliation, Condent exercised unusual restraint over his crew and prevented the torturing of any prisoners to avoid exacerbating the situation.[259]

Condent returned to the island of Saint Marie off the coast of Madagascar, where the huge fortune they had seized was divided among the crew. The average share was approximately 2,000 English pounds. While some of the crewmembers elected to settle among the Madagascar natives, forty went with Condent to the island of Reunion where they sought an official pardon from the French Governor for their actions. With the aid of a sizable bribe, the pardons were obtained. Condent then courted and won the hand of the Governor's daughter (or sister-in-law, according to your source of information). The couple went to France, where they settled in Brittany,[260] and Condent became a successful, obviously wealthy merchant. In his latter years he seemingly mellowed, since there are no public records of neighbors or business rivals losing their noses or ears.

Chapter Eighteen: Edward England, Proof That
No Good Deed Goes Unpunished

*E*dward England was born Edward Seegar in Ireland, probably near the end of the seventeenth century or early in the eighteenth.[261] As is usually the case with pirates of presumed humble origins, even this sketchy description of his early background is difficult to confirm with hard facts.

By 1717, Seegar was pursuing his seafaring career as a mate onboard a merchant sloop operating out of the port of Jamaica. His ship was captured later that year by a pirate named Christopher Winter. When he was given the opportunity to join the pirate crew, he readily accepted. Seegar did change his last name to England, though, perhaps to conceal his real identity and make it easier to return to his homeland once his buccaneering career was over.[262]

England quickly adapted to the pirate lifestyle, and proved to be a valuable member of Winter's crew. Like so many other pirates, he seemed to thrive in New Providence, Bahamas, which was Winter's home base of operations. His newlifestyle was to undergo a marked change in July of 1718 with the arrival of the new Governor, Woodes Rogers. As Rogers began to assert some control over pirateering through liberal granting of one-time pardons, England elected to flee New Providence in a stolen sloop and strike out on his own.[263]

He sailed along the African coast, traveling from the Azores to the Cape Verde Islands where he and his crew prospered, seizing a number of ships, looting some, burning others, and converting the remainder into pirate vessels. One of the larger captured ships, the *Pearl,* was renamed the *Royal James* and retained as the flagship of England's small fleet.[264] Some historians ignore the name change and continue to refer to England's flagship as the *Pearl.* England and his crew continued their passage along the African coast, collecting a large number of prizes. England retained one of these prizes, the sloop *Victory,* to enlarge his fleet. He placed his first mate, John Taylor, in command of the *Victory,*[265] and the small fleet went on sailing around the Horn of Africa. After passing into the Indian Ocean, they again added to their list of captured prizes, including a 34-gun, square-rigged Dutchman, which England called the *Fancy* and made over into his newest flagship.[267]

On April 27, 1720, England and Taylor were approaching a harbor in Madagascar, when they encountered three ships from the East India Trading Company -- two English and one Dutch. While the two smaller vessels attempted to elude the pirates, the largest, the *Cassandra* commanded by a Scot, James Macrae, took on the *Fancy* and thereby provided some degree of cover for the two remaining East Indiamen.[268] Taylor pursued the two fleeing vessels while England and Macrae exchanged broadside after broadside at close range for over three hours. The devastation on board both vessels was tremendous. The *Fancy* suffered ninety causalities, while the *Cassandra* reported thirty-seven according to her captain.[268] The onslaught continued; but the Scottish Captain eventually realized that the better-equipped pirates were getting the upper hand in the struggle and ran the *Cassandra* aground on the beach. He and his few remaining crew retreated and went into hiding. When the pirates stormed the beached *Cassandra*, they found an exceedingly valuable cargo reportedly worth 75,000 English pounds.[269]

After over a week of hiding, Macrae and his remaining crew were near death due to lack of food and water. Reluctantly, they concluded that they had no choice but to surrender to Captain England and his men. Although England was willing to release the prisoners from the onset, most of his men were not so favorably disposed. This was particularly true of Captain Taylor, who clearly wanted revenge for his lost compatriots. England prevailed but was to pay a terrible price for his act of kindliness.[270] Taylor eventually persuaded the crew to depose England; and in early 1721, they marooned him and three supporters on a small island near Madagascar.[271] England or Seegar and his few loyal men were eventually able to build a raft and somehow reach the shores of Madagascar. Unfortunately, England was forced to beg from fellow pirates for food to live and died in poverty shortly thereafter.[272]

Chapter Nineteen: William Fly, the Shortest Pirate Career

$\mathcal{W}$illiam Fly bears the distinction of having one of the shortest, if not the shortest, pirate careers in history. He terrorized the seas from May 27 to his hanging on July 12, 1727: a career of somewhere between one and two months.

Zepke[273] suggests that he may have been a prizefighter before pursuing a life on the sea, apparently attracted to a career change by the possibility of finally earning his fortune. Given his reputed furious temper, foul mouth, and his marked tendency towards cruelty, it is not difficult to visualize him initially being drawn into the prize ring.   Whatever the reason, he was probably not very well if at all educated, or particularly bright, and certainly not known for his seamanship skills.

In April, 1726, he was hired as a boatswain or petty officer in charge of the deck force and work crews on board the slaver *Elizabeth* by its Captain, James Green. The *Elizabeth*, which originated out of Bristol, was on route from Jamaica to Guinea in May of 1727 when as often seemed to be the case in this trade, Fly provoked a mutiny against his master. He had the crew wait until their captain had retired in a drunken state and then had him dragged up on deck. Ignoring Green's pleas to be allowed to join the crew, be put ashore, or at least make his last confession, Fly had him thrown overboard. Somehow Captain Green managed to grab hold of the mainsail and retain his grip. One of Fly's crew responded by seizing an ax and cutting off the former captain's hand.[274] Next, Green's loyal first mate, Thomas Jenkins, was forced up on deck. He struggled vigorously with his adversaries until one of the pirate crew attempted to behead him with an ax, missed, and removed a large chunk of his shoulder instead. He met the same fate as his captain.[275]

During his brief and unprofitable career as a pirate, Fly raided merchant shipping along the coasts of North Carolina and New England. His first victim was a merchantman, the *John and Hannah*, which apparently ran aground on a sandbar off the North Carolina coast.[276] When its captain was unable to free her in response to Fly's demand, Fly flew into a rage, conscripted the captain, had him severely beaten, and set the merchantman on fire out of spite.[277]

The usual booty from these "prizes" consisted of items such as small weapons and extra sails. In addition, several new crewmembers were conscripted, including a skilled and clever navigator named Atkinson.[278] Atkinson had no desire to become a pirate, so he ingratiated himself to the pirate crew and bided his time, waiting for an opportunity to escape. The opportunity came about on the coast of Nantucket where they captured a fishing vessel off Browning's Bank. Fly ordered the majority of his crew into the fishing vessel to pursue another schooner, while he, three other pirates, and fifteen conscripts remained behind. Realizing that Fly and his few remaining crewmembers were badly outnumbered, Atkinson and his captured compatriots took the pirates prisoner, and fled before the rest of Fly's crew returned in the fishing vessel.[279]

Fly and his companions were then transported to Great Brewster, which they reached on June 28, and turned over as prisoners to the proper authorities. The pirates were tried at Boston courthouse on July 4, found guilty of piracy, and sentenced to be hanged on July 12.[280]

According to several sources, Fly was completely disdainful of the actual hanging. Supposedly, he even chastised the executioner for doing a poor job tying the hangman's knot, remaking the noose and placing it about his neck with his own two hands."[281] Now that's what one might well call a pirate's pirate -- albeit not a particularly bright one.

Chapter Twenty: William "Billy" Lewis, the Devil's Disciple

*W*illiam "Billy" Lewis was an American who was so fluent in both English and French that historians are still uncertain of his true ancestry.[282] He was also conversant in Spanish and a number of obscure native dialects. By the age of eleven he was sailing out of Boston harbor under the tutelage of pirate Captain Banister. During this period he met and formed a lifelong friendship with another youthful crewmember named Darby McCaffrey. Eventually the British navy captured Banister's ship and the entire crew was turned over for trial in Port Royal, Jamaica. Lewis, because of his age, was able to secure his release and that of his friend by claiming that they had been forced into service against their will.[283]

The two boys, now free, elected to become members of the crew of a merchantman, and spent the next several years honing their skills as seamen. This adventure was not destined to last, however, and Spanish pirates in Havana eventually captured their ship. This event resulted in an obvious change in their lifestyle. Forced into servitude by the pirates, they were subjected to tremendous cruelty, backbreaking work, and insufficient quantities of wretched food. Unable to endure these deplorable conditions for long, Lewis, McCaffrey, and six other disgusted members of the crew escaped. They stole a canoe, which they gradually replaced with progressively larger ships and bigger and bigger crews. Eventually, Billy Lewis was elected the captain of a 40-gun large schooner, which he had renamed the *Morning Star*. Darby McCaffrey was appointed his quartermaster.[284] The pirates, while still quite young, were already well known and feared throughout the region. As the author of *Career Pirate from Nassau* colorfully states "…he was still a young captain and his actions [had already] thrust him into the hierarchy of the Brethren of the Coast."[285]

Lewis' greatest victory may well have been, ironically, the cause of his greatest loss and ultimate undoing. He and his crew came upon a large French man-of-war that they clearly had no chance of capturing in a direct confrontation. Instead, they waited patiently until two small boats were dispatched from the Frenchman in search of a fresh catch of fish. Lewis seized the two fishing boats, replacing their crew with his own men and instructing them to return to the French man-of-war. As he had anticipated, the French assumed them to be their comrades returning from a fishing expedition and allowed them to board the vessel without any challenge. Once the pirates boarded the French man-of-war, a long and fierce struggle ensued. At the conclusion of the battle, Lewis emerged successfully and became the captain of a pirate fleet of over two hundred crewmen. However, he had paid a terrible price for his victory, for his lifelong friend Darby had been killed in the struggle.[286]

From this time forward, Lewis' personality and behavior appeared to undergo significant changes. He seemed to spend a great deal of time muttering to himself, or, as his crew increasingly believed, to someone else, such as the Devil. According to Terrance Zepke, his behavior also became more and more erratic.[287] He had enjoyed a remarkably long career, and it wasn't until sometime in 1727 that it finally came to a close. The *Morning Star* was in pursuit of a schooner off the coast of South Carolina when incoming fire broke off the tops of two of the *Morning Star's* main masts and forced her to lose speed. The pursuit seemed to be at an end when Billy Lewis climbed what remained of his main mast, tore out a clump of his hair, and shouted for the Devil to take his offering of hair until it was time for him to be taken himself by the Devil.[288] Some regard this crazed behavior almost as a perverted prayer to the Devil for more speed. Certainly, many members of his crew did. In any event, the ship suddenly did pick up speed: enough speed in fact to overtake the fleeing schooner, which they soon captured.

Needless to say, the superstitious crew quickly concluded that William Lewis must be a disciple of the Devil. Some of his loyal crew members tried to warn him of the extreme fear he had aroused and, as a result, of the perilous position in which he had placed his own life. Lewis ignored these warnings, essentially saying that the Devil would come for him that night, and that nothing could be done about it.[289] Evidently, a majority of the terrified crew reportedly drew straws that night, and one crewmember was selected to slip into Lewis' cabin while he was sleeping and dispatch him with a pistol shot.[290]

Now, many of the more notorious pirate captains were believed by at least some of their crewmembers to have a special relationship with the Devil. For example, Edward Teach was also known as the "Fury from Hell", and his cultivated, demonic appearance did nothing to dissuade those who suspected that he might have made a pact with the Devil. Once again, my favorite resource, Terrance Zepke, reports that members of his crew claimed that he could be seen on deck or down in the hold talking to someone who was definitely not a crew member … someone who would suddenly disappear. However, William Lewis was the only pirate captain to bring about his own end by his too frequently and publicly expressed belief in the Devil.

Lewis' story makes an interesting background for the most thoughtful question I have ever have ever had to address after making a presentation to an audience. A young lady somewhere between the ages of nine and eleven asked: Did pirates believe in God?

On the surface, most would think that the correct answer would be no. However, in most cases, I think that just the opposite may have been true. Remember that pirates were fatalistic about their own futures, and with good cause. They knew, with as close to absolute certainty as one could come in their world, that their deaths would be violent and soon. Recall that the average pirate's career only lasted from one to three years.

But even one of the most notorious pirates of the early Golden Age, "Black Bart" Roberts, drew up a Pirate Code, a contract for his crew, that at least indirectly acknowledged a belief in a Supreme Being. One of its provisions specified the ship's musicians could not be forced to play music on the Sabbath Day. So, I think it wasn't the case that most pirates didn't believe in God, but instead, that they were already resigned to a short life span and, perhaps, to eternal damnation. Remember that the Christian churches of the early seventeen hundreds placed much more emphasis on punishment for sins, Hell, and eternal damnation than their modern counterparts, which tend to stress God's love, repentance, and forgiveness.

Chapter Twenty-one: John Paul Jones, English Pirate and Father of the American Navy

*J*ohn Paul Jones, who is generally regarded as the father of the American Navy, is a much more complex individual than we typically learn about in American history books. For example, even though he is one of our greatest heroes, he never became a citizen of his adopted country, and while much admired by the ladies in general – an admiration that he enthusiastically returned -- he never married.

John Paul Jones was born John Paul in his father's cottage, a poor gardener on a Scottish estate in Kirkcudbright, on July 6, 1747. [291] By the age of thirteen, he was apprenticed as a cabin boy in the British merchant marine brig, *Friendship,* so that he could learn the seafaring trade.[292]

His career was rapidly propelled forward by his obvious skill and daring, and in 1769 he was appointed to his first command as captain of the brig *John.* Four years later he was supposedly involved in an episode that was to mark the remainder of his life. He had completed the first half of a trading venture to the Caribbean island of Tobago on the *Betsy,* when he made the fateful decision to forbid shore leave and to use the crew's shore leave pay to purchase cargo for the return trip. The ringleader of the crew attempted to go on the forbidden shore leave. He attacked John Paul with a bludgeon when the captain challenged his departure, and John Paul ran him through with his sword, killing him instantly. He then went ashore and turned himself in to the local authorities, awaiting a formal hearing on the incident. Unfortunately. the dead sailor had been quite popular, and there was a great deal of general hostility generated against John Paul. This resentment was so pronounced that his friends advised him to escape from prison and flee to his older brother's estate in Fredericksburg, Virginia. He took their advice and as a result, the British forever labeled him as a pirate. The fact that he was born in Scotland but attacked British ports, shipping and naval vessels during the American Revolution probably did nothing to alter this opinion. Sir Winston Churchill referred to him as a privateer, as opposed to an enemy combatant, in his historical writings, even though John Paul never had a privateer's Letter of Marque. The adoption of his surname "Jones" was an effort to make his identity harder to ascertain in case the British ever apprehended him.

In 1775, following the outbreak of the American Revolution, Jones went to Philadelphia and was the first individual to be commissioned a

Lieutenant in the Continental Navy. As a lieutenant on board the *Alfred*, he was also the first American naval officer to raise the Grand Union flag.[293] According to the Naval History Center of the Department of the Navy, "the flag's Union Jack in the upper left canton and thirteen red and white stripes represented a united resistance to tyranny but loyalty to the English King."[294]

On May 10th of the following year, Jones was given command of the twelve-gun sloop *Providence* and received his commission as a captain in the Continental Navy on August 8. During his initial voyage, Jones captured sixteen British prizes and destroyed the British fisheries in Nova Scotia. He also avoided capture by the 28-gun frigate *Solebay* through the exercise of brilliant seamanship during a ten-hour pursuit. Jones later stated that he regarded this voyage as the most enjoyable and rewarding of his career. He also thought highly of his crew, considering it the most skilled with which he had ever sailed.[295] The British were undoubtedly less enthusiastic.

Unfortunately, John Paul Jones may have been more gifted as a seaman than he was as a diplomat. After returning to Boston on December 16, 1776, he is reputed to have had several disagreements with some of his superiors. As a result, this man whom many historians have labeled "the Father of the American Navy", was never to rise above the rank of captain in service to that same navy.[296]

On June 14, 1777, he was appointed captain of the eighteen-gun frigate *USS Ranger*.[297] On the first of November of that same year, he set sail for France with a charge to attack British shipping and to provide whatever aid he could to the American side. At this juncture he could only offer strategic advice to the American commissioners in France -- Benjamin Franklin, John Adams, and Henry Lee – since France was still maintaining an official role of neutrality in the American-British conflict. The commissioners apparently were responsive to his input, and Jones formed a close, personal relationship with Franklin as a result of their interaction.

France formally recognized American independence through a Treaty of Alliance that was signed on February 6, 1778.[298] As a result, Jones' long period of inactivity in France was finally at an end; and eight days after the signing of the agreement, Jones became the first American Navy officer to be saluted by the French.[299]

Jones sailed from Brest, France, on April 17 to renew his harassment of the British. After a series of minor adventures and misadventures, Jones fought an hour-long battle with the 20-gun sloop *Drake* on April 24 off the coast of Carrickfergus, Ireland.[300] By defeating the *Drake* and killing her captain, Jones earned one of the few American naval victories of the Revolutionary War. Unfortunately, the victory was somewhat marred by a bitter dispute between

Jones and his first mate, Lieutenant Simpson. Jones had Simpson arrested when they returned to port in France, but Commissioner Adams intervened and ordered his release.[301]

Fortunately, Jones' popularity with the French was unaffected by the Simpson situation. The following year, the Americans were either given or loaned (depending on your historical source) a fourteen year-old East Indian merchantman originally known as the *Duc de Duras*[302] to be placed under the command of John Paul Jones. He converted the *Duras* into a 40-gun warship, which he renamed the *Bonhomme Richard*.[303] The *less heavily armed, French commanded Alliance, Pallas, Vengeance, and Cerf to form a small naval squadron accompanied the Bonhomme Richard.*[304]

On September 23, 1779, Jones and his squadron encountered a British merchant fleet off the coast of Flamborough Head in Yorkshire. Two British warships, the newly built 50-gun *Serapis* and the 20-gun *Countess of Scarborough*, protected the merchantmen.[305] The primary engagement was the one that ensued between the largest American and British men-of-war. The *Bonhomme Richard* bore the early brunt of this 3-4 hour long battle. She absorbed a number of direct hits below her waterline that would eventually cause her to sink. Additionally, her main battery exploded, destroying much of the upper deck as well as setting it on fire. The *Serapis* attempted to sail across the American's bow in order to rake her. In the process, the British captain noticed the absence of a large portion of the main mast and the American ensign. He called out to Jones, asking if the Americans had struck their colors, a traditional sign of surrender. Jones' reply of "I have not yet begun to fight" will remain forever in the hearts and minds of all Americans. Jones then maneuvered his sinking ship alongside the *Serapis* and lashed the two vessels together with grappling lines. After his marines' withering fire cleared the enemy's deck of sailors, Jones' remaining cannons weakened the British vessel's main mast, and Captain Pearson surrendered. As the *Bonhomme Richard* sank, Jones and his crew took possession of the *Serapis,* bringing to a close one of the earliest and greatest victories in American naval history, and the first American defeat ever of a British warship in British waters.[306]

John Paul Jones was nowhere more celebrated than in France, England's historical enemy. King Louis had him made a Chevalier, inducted him into the Ordre du Merite Militaire, and presented him with a ceremonial sword. He was also initiated into the French Legion d'Honneur. The U.S. Congress had a gold medal struck in his honor commemorating his "valor and brilliant services". The medal was awarded to the "Chevalier John Paul Jones" according to his expressed wishes.

Nevertheless, he was never to hold a major American naval position again. Following the conclusion of the Revolutionary War, Jones was assigned the duty of returning to Europe to collect prize money due his crew from their exploits during the War.

His military exploits were not over, however. In 1788, Empress Catherine the Great recruited John Paul Jones to join the Russian navy. He was commissioned as a rear admiral and assigned to the Black Sea theater, where he played a prominent role in repulsing the Turks.[307] As had been the case in America, however, Jones had jealous but influential rivals in the Russian court who attacked Jones' character, going so far as to accuse him of having an affair with an underage girl.[308] As a result, John Paul Jones was recalled to St. Petersberg and essentially forced into a life of idleness. Soon he left the court in disgust and returned to Paris.[309]

In 1792 Jones was appointed U.S. Consul to Algiers with the task of securing the release of American prisoners. Before he could undertake his mission, however, he died face down in his bed on July 18. He was buried in a lead-lined coffin in the Parisian St. Louis Cemetery for Alien Protestants.[310] Four years later, the revolutionary government that had replaced the French monarchy sold the cemetery, and it went on to serve a variety of purposes including a burial ground for dead animals and an arena for animal fighting.

In 1905, over one hundred years later, the cemetery and Jones' special coffin were identified after a six-year search by a team headed by the U.S. Ambassador to France, General Horace Porter.[311] Jones' body was formally removed from the onetime cemetery and returned with full military honors to the United States.[312] President Theodore Roosevelt presided over Jones interment at the U.S. Naval Academy Chapel on April 24, 1906.[313] A portion of his speech is reproduced below:[314]

> The future naval officers, who live within these walls, will find in the career of the man whose life this day we celebrate, not merely a subject for admiration and respect, but an object lesson to be taken into their inner-most hearts. Every officer…should feel in each fiber of his being an eager desire to emulate the energy, the professional capacity, the indomitable determination and dauntless scorn of death, which marked John Paul Jones above all his fellows.

Chapter Twenty-two: Jean Lafitte, Villain or American Hero?

*H*aving grown up as a landlocked Midwesterner in Indianapolis, Indiana, I only knew of two pirates by name -- Long John Silver of *Treasure Island* fame and Jean Lafitte. In my mind, Lafitte was the ideal of a dashing pirate and looked remarkably like Yul Brenner, who played the pirate in the 1958 movie *The Buccaneer.* On the silver screen, Brenner/Lafitte displayed all of the noble characteristics demanded of any teenaged male's heroes; in short, he was popular with the ladies. As I vaguely remembered the story line of the movie, he also had something to do with the Battle of New Orleans.

Lafitte's legend has been celebrated in many ways, not only in the movies. Several books have been written about him, and the immortal Lord Byron celebrated him with the famous lines:[315]

> He left a corsair's name to other times,
> linked one virtue to a thousand crimes.

At the other extreme, his character made friends with "Hoss Cartwright" on an episode of the television series *Bonanza,* and he has also appeared on "Cap'n Crunch" cereal commercials as the villainous pirate "Jean Lafoote".

Despite this notoriety, as little is known about Lafitte's early history as was known of the other buccaneers considered in this work. According to most historians, he was reputedly most likely born between 1780-1782 in Port-au-Prince, Haiti, or Bayonne, France (to mention a few of the more popularly reputed locations) to a French father and a Spanish mother.[316] Legend asserts that Lafitte's family was originally Jewish but forced to convert to Catholicism under the Spanish Inquisition sometime during the 1490s. Religious persecution may have been the primary reason for the family's migration from Spain to France and, ultimately, to the New World. Lafitte's maternal grandfather was presumably martyred for his Jewish beliefs. Unfortunately, this early family history is based on Lafitte's own personal journal, a source that has fallen under suspicion in recent times, and other sources of similarly questionable authenticity.

In any event, Jean Lafitte and his older brother Pierre had established a New Orleans blacksmith business by 1809. The blacksmith business was actually a cover for an extremely broad and successful smuggling operation.[317]

The smuggling operation dealt in captured slaves and other contraband stolen from Spanish trading vessels by a loose confederation of pirates. Not surprisingly, the Lafitte brothers reputedly owned considerable shares in this confederation. Jean apparently was primarily responsible for the naval operations, while Pierre focused more on day-to-day business transactions.

Since the importation of slaves had been banned in the United States by a Congressional compromise, the legislation upon which the ban was based had given rise to an underground enterprise to fill the need for additional slave labor in states such as Louisiana. As a result, business thrived.[318] Business was so good, in fact, that it came to the attention of Louisiana's Governor Claiborne, who had the brothers arrested on charges of piracy and illegal trading.[319] With the assistance of some of the best-known lawyers in the area, the brothers were released on bond and soon escaped into the swamps and bayous south of the city.[320] The Governor reacted by placing a bounty of $500 on each of the Lafitte brother's heads.[321] Jean Lafitte responded characteristically by offering a ($1,500 - $5,000, depending on your source) reward for the head of the Governor.[322]

Once the Lafitte brothers were safely established in their new home in the wilderness, which they dubbed the Kingdom of Barataria,[323] they quickly resumed their highly successful smuggling operation. One of their better-known trading partners was rumored to have been another famous Louisianan, Jim Bowie.

During this same era, the long-standing, bitter feud between Great Britain and the United States over the former nation's assumed rights on the high seas boiled over into open war. First, the British repulsed an American invasion of Canada. Next, they succeeded in bottling up most of the young nation's fledgling navy in its homeports. The British invaders then landed in Maryland, attacked the Capitol just hours behind the fleeing President, and burned the White House.

On September 3, 1814, the British warship HMS *Sophia* contacted Lafitte in the Gulf of Mexico. The King's representatives offered the Baratarians both British citizenship and American land holdings in return for their assistance in the conflict with America. Refusal would likely have ensured the destruction of Barataria by the British navy.[324]

Lafitte requested fifteen days to consider the British offer, quickly made copies of the British letters, and sent them to Jean Blanque, a comrade and member of the Louisiana legislature. Shortly thereafter, Lafitte pledged his support to New Orleans should it ever be threatened by the British, and his formerly imprisoned brother, Pierre, mysteriously "escaped" from confinement.

In early 1815 Britain attempted to finalize its campaign against the United States by invading New Orleans and seizing control of the Mississippi River and its commercial traffic. However, they clearly had not given enough consideration to the capability of Andrew Jackson, the American commander, and his ally Jean Lafitte. Lafitte forever inscribed his name in the annals of American history by pledging the support of his men to Jackson's forces. Estimates of the size of this contribution range from a few dozen to more than 3,000. More important than their number, however, was their background, for all were fierce fighters and many were skilled artillerists. The two sides clashed on January 8, 1815, and a bloody battle ensued in which the British were decimated.[325] Shortly after the battle, President Madison offered a full pardon to all of Lafitte's privateers or pirates who had participated in the conflict, and many accepted. In contrast, their leader declined and headed for Texas to resume his lawless ways.[326]

The last years of the Lafitte brothers' story, like their early days, are short on documentation and long on rumor and folklore. It seems likely that they succeeded in establishing a new operations center in Galveston, to which they attracted a number of privateers and pirates. While they prospered initially, they are reputed to have departed from their previous code and attacked American trading vessels. In retaliation, the United States government sent a warship to Galveston, forcing the Lafittes to flee. Other rumors imply that during this same period, the Lafittes served as agents for the Spanish government and, perhaps, the United States as well.

The escape from Galveston marked the beginning of the rapid decline of the Lafitte brothers' fate. Shortly thereafter, Pierre is reported to have died at sea.

Jean's end is even less certain. Reduced to the status of impoverished minor pirate, he may have contracted some fearsome tropical disease and succumbed in a poor native hut, or may have died at sea of wounds he received acting as a privateer. Some even believe he may have returned to his adopted country and lived out his life under an assumed name.[327,328]

In the end, the answer to the question raised in the title of this chapter may well have been "both". If so, Lord Byron seems to have stated it both elegantly and succinctly.

Mike Hogan

PART II:
THE PETTICOAT PIRATES

*T*horoughly Irish as I am, I have always had a real fondness for members of the fairer sex. That said, it is not surprising that my favorite buccaneers of all time were the petticoat pirates of the Golden Age. It has been estimated that as few as 0.5%,[329] or one out of every two hundred pirates were women in that era. Why were there so few of them? Well, we have already seen that it was very difficult if not impossible to live life on one's own terms as a male in the seventeenth and eighteenth centuries. Can you even begin to imagine what it would have been like to achieve this same level of independence as a woman, particularly as a pirate? You would have had to have been as adept in battle as any of your male compatriots. Moreover, since it was generally a violation of the standard buccaneer code or contract for a woman to be on board a pirate ship, any aspiring female pirate would have needed to adopt a convincing male persona and maintain it at all times.

This need for deception offers us a second possible explanation for the apparent scarcity of women pirates; our inability to know with certainty which pirates may have, in fact, been female. You must bear in mind that in the 1600's and 1700's, neither men nor women bathed regularly. Nor did members of the same sex appear in front of each other in the nude. For these reasons, concealment of one's sex would undoubtedly have been easier to accomplish back in those days.

Finally, the male ego being what it is, historians have often downplayed or outright ignored the contributions of female pirates, particularly the so-called pirate queens.

Cathy Converse, the lecturer on "The Lady Was A Pirate," has summarized my feelings about petticoat pirates much more effectively than I ever could:[330]

> These were women of strength, wit, courage, ambition, and astonishing resourcefulness…but they were also common thieves, plunderers, ruthless, and vicious. They stole, maimed, and killed. I don't think I would have wanted to have known any of the women I have discussed tonight.

Chapter Twenty-three: Alfhild, the Viking Princess

*I*n the Introduction to this section on Petticoat Pirates, I enumerated some of the many problems associated with identifying female buccaneers, not the least of which was the fact that they usually concealed themselves behind an assumed male persona. If we go even further back in time -- at least another 800-900 years -- to the days of the Vikings, who ruled the seas for nearly three centuries, the problem becomes much more complicated. First, the Vikings indiscriminately mingled history with myth in their story telling, and story telling was the way they passed on their history from one generation to the next. The tale of Alfhild (aka. Alvilda, Alwilda, or Alvild)[331] the Swedish princess, is a perfect illustration of this oral tradition. Next, most Vikings would never have considered themselves to be pirates. Instead, they saw themselves as simple farmers, merchants, or craftsmen. They only went plundering or *i viking*[331] to supplement their income. They favored villages with large churches and/or monasteries to steal gold, silver and other precious metals and to take captives for later trade, sale, or entertainment such as drowning at sea. So, historical references to petticoat pirates among the Vikings are indeed rare.

The story of Princess Alfhild, daughter of Synardus, the King of the Goths,[333] who was supposedly born no earlier than 850 AD, is a case in point. Like most noble women of her era she is said to have worn a heavy hood at all times in public to conceal her face from and avoid arousing the interests of potential male admirers. Furthermore, her parents may have kept her locked in her bedroom to keep her safe. Nevertheless, the story of her striking blond hair and great beauty was well known throughout the land, and she didn't suffer from a lack of suitors. To make the competition for her hand more challenging and to avoid having her marry and leave them for as long as possible, her father is said to have imposed two obstacles in the path of her potential suitors. He placed two guards at the door of her bedroom chamber[334] – a poisonous snake and a viper, or two dragons, depending on your source.

Nevertheless, many suitors are reported to have tried and failed until Prince Alf, son of Sigar, King of Denmark, took this quest upon himself.[335] According to two different versions of the story, Alf faced the two snake or the two dragon sentries, and successfully slew the guardians of the bedchamber. Before he could knock on the bedchamber door, however, Alfhild presumably acted on the advice of her mother, who was opposed to any male taking her daughter away. Accordingly, Alfhid decided to "avoid marrying some stuffy prince" by changing into man's clothing, fleeing the castle, and escaping to sea as a pirate.[336] While she reputedly went to sea initially with an all female (cross dressing) crew, they soon encountered another pirate ship that had recently lost its captain. The pirate crew was so impressed with Alfhid's many abilities that they elected her their new leader and combined their two crews.[337] The newly enlarged crew met with great success under her fierce leadership, and reputedly attained a number of important victories, particularly over the Danes. Yet, she and her crew were eventually attacked in the Gulf of Finland and bested for the first time by the Danes and Prince Alf, who was trying to rid the area of buccaneers. According to one version of the tale, he was dueling with her and about to put her to the sword, when he accidentally dislodged her helmet and suddenly recognized the beautiful face of his beloved. Although there is no record of their conversation following this event, it apparently was quite friendly since they were soon married on board his ship[339] She became his Queen, and bore him a beautiful daughter named Gurit.[340]

While many researchers regard Alfhild's tale as strictly fictional, I feel that it is difficult to say so with any certainty after one dismisses the nature and role of the bedchamber guardians and notes the number of historical names and events that support the tale. Furthermore, similar uncertainty may be associated with other presumed Viking pirate notables such as Princess Sela (420 AD), Princess Rusia (Russila) and her sister Stikla, Wigbiorg (800s AD), and Hetha (800s AD).

Finally, since I am both Irish and somewhat, perhaps even too, romantic by nature, I have always given some credibility to so-called fairy tales. Almost every fairy tale has at least a little basis in fact. Besides, since I firmly believe in the wee little people and their three magical wishes or pots of gold, it is only a short step for me from them to the land of fairy tales.

Chapter Twenty-four: Lady Mary (Elizabeth) Killigrew, a Pirate in Disguise

*I*n Elizabethan England (1558–1603), the distinction between pirates and privateers was frequently blurred, as is illustrated by the life of Sir Francis Drake. What might be regarded as a shocking plundering at sea could also be viewed as an almost harmless or an essentially legitimate effort to expand one's wealth, depending on the times, individuals and countries involved in the incident. John Killigrew and his charming wife Mary adapted readily to this interesting life style.[341]

Lady Killigrew of Cornwall was a member of the highly respected Killigrew clan, of which her husband, Sir John, was titular head.[342] She was also the daughter of a well-known Suffolk pirate of the day, who undoubtedly taught his high-spirited daughter much about the trade at an early age.[343] The Killigrews owned Arwenach Castle, an imposing structure at the mouth of Falmouth Harbor, where they frequently entertained the highest members of the nobility.

Sir John and his wife supported their lavish lifestyle in part through partnership with a syndicate of pirates in coastal England who plundered merchant shipping and supplied the Killigrews with the goods that they had stolen. The Pettigrew's would, in turn, act as fences for the stolen property and provide their accomplices with the appropriate shares for their activities. During this same period, Sir John took on the role of fox in the hen house, so to speak, and accepted an appointment as Vice-Admiral of Cornwall, England. He was officially charged with ridding southwest England of pirates.

While he was away on various missions, Lady Pettigrew filled her free time by honing her skills as a pirate in disguise.[344] There are number of different versions of the event that finally brought her pirating days to an end. According to this particular version, a Spanish trading vessel, the *Maria*, tied up at Falmouth Harbor on January 1, 1583,[345] to ride out a particularly violent storm of several days duration. Lady Pettigrew had members of her household staff, whom she had impressed as her part-time crew, check out the merchantman under cover of darkness. When they returned and assured her that indeed the ship contained a rich cargo, she invited the Spanish captain and first lieutenant to visit Arwenach Castle as her guests while they were delayed by the foul weather. They immediately accepted and were soon charmed by the luxury of their surroundings and the beauty of their elegant hostess. Following a particularly lavish dinner, Lady Killigrew excused herself for a short time, went downstairs where her household crew awaited her, and quietly rowed out to the *Maria*. After killing everyone who was still onboard, she and her crew presumably emptied the ship of all its treasures (although there is no definitive proof that she went on board and, therefore, qualified as a pirate per se). While her crew took the ship itself for resale, Lady Killigrew returned to her castle, changed back into her fine gown, and continued entertaining her guests until everyone retired for the evening.[346] When the Spaniards found their ship to be missing, they immediately requested a local investigation of the incident, though nothing ever came of the matter.[347]

Another version of the story claims that, unfortunately, this result apparently so emboldened our heroine that next she attacked a German vessel that similarly sought refuge in Falmouth Harbor. Presumably, as before, she apparently killed the entire German crew and made off with the ship's very valuable cargo, which included precious metals and jewels.[348] This time, the German ship was essentially under the protection of the Queen,[349] who had Lady Killigrew and crew arrested and tried. They were convicted and sentenced to death, Just before the sentence was to be executed, Elizabeth pardoned Lady Killigrew, perhaps recognizing her potential worth to the Queen.

Regardless of which version of her tale is the correct one, the good Lady did finally abandon her exciting life of piracy and returned to her more mundane role of fencing stolen property.

Chapter 25: Grace O'Malley, Pirate Queen of Ireland

race O'Malley was born in 1530 on Clare Island in County Mayo, Ireland.[350] She was the daughter of Owen "Black Oak" O'Malley, head of the seafaring O'Malley clan, which had actively traded with Spain and Scotland since the eleven hundreds.[351] During this era, Great Britain was slowly but methodically taking control of much of Ireland by "offering" English titles and an end to hostilities to various clan chieftains in return for control of their property through a process known as "Submit and Regrant." The O'Malleys were among the Irish clans that most vigorously resisted this British encroachment.

Grace's mother had been determined that her young daughter would grow up to be the lady to which she was destined because of her elevated position in the O'Malley clan. She made certain that Grace had a strong education, which included a fluency in Latin.[352] But these efforts were to no avail. Grace was drawn to the sea and the careers of her father and male ancestors. She cut off her hair, dressed like a boy, and attempted to board one of her father's ships sailing to Spain. While her father and brother laughingly referred to her as "Grainne Mhaol", Gaelic for "Bald Grace",[353] and returned her to shore, it wasn't long before she was to join them in their travels.

On one of these early journeys the story is told that Grace had been ordered to go below deck at the first sign of danger. Instead, she disobeyed those instructions and climbed up the main sail's rigging when English pirates besieged her father's ship. As Grace watched spellbound from the rigging, she saw the tide of battle turn against her father and his crew. When an English pirate sneaked up behind her father and prepared to stab him, Grace, still more of a child than a woman, screamed out a warning to alert him to the impending danger. Then she dived from the rigging, still screaming all the while, and landed on the pirate's back, disabling him. Her actions undoubtedly saved her father's life and allowed him and his crew to regain control of their ship.[354] This was the first recorded example of her courage and resourcefulness.

At the age of sixteen, Grace's marriage was arranged to Donal O'Flaherty, who was tainist or next in line to be chieftain of the ancestral O'Flaherty clan.[355] Donal, who was also known as Donal-an-Chogaidh[356] (or Donald of the Battles), was supposed to have a vicious temper and was renowned for his skill in battle. He was even reputed to have murdered his sister's stepson to prevent him from becoming a political rival within the clan. While their marriage was originally spawned by political convenience, they appeared to have been devoted to each other during their nineteen years of married life. Grace bore Donal three children: a daughter, Margaret and two sons, Owen and Murrough, the last of whom is said to have little regard for women and even plotted to have his older brother murdered by the British. Grace was never to speak to him again after her beloved Owen's death.[357] She also took an active role in the clan, becoming a shrewd politician, able seaman, and a genuine leader of men. Recognizing her outstanding abilities, the clan soon placed her in charge of their fleet of ships. She excelled relative to her husband in almost every aspect of clan life.

Donal's infamous temper finally proved to be his undoing, and he was killed by a rival clan member when Grace was 35. Although she was entitled to one-third of his holdings as his widow under clan law, the O'Flaherty's reneged on their contractual obligations and gave her nothing. Grace took her three children and 200 loyal followers and returned to her ancestral home on Clare Island with her fellow O'Malleys.[358] Still imbued with her great love of the sea and her strong sense of adventure and daring, she quickly rose to prominence and wealth again through fishing, trade, and, eventually, as the pirate queen of western Ireland.

Shortly after Donal's death, Grace, or Granuaile[359] as she was often known, went to Castle Rockfleet, knocked on the door, and proposed a one-year marriage to the castle owner, Richard "Iron Dick" Burke, as a political alliance against the growing expansion of British rule. While Burke readily accepted her offer, he became quite enamored with the beautiful woman that Grace was, and definitely refused her "no-fault release" at the end of their first year of marriage. She bore him one son, Theobald, and they remained faithful to each other until his death some sixteen years later.[360]

During her prolonged career as Ireland's pirate queen, Grace was renowned for her tactical skills and her ferocity in battle. She often fought with a sword in each hand, and was well known for her hatred of cowardliness. During a particularly bloody battle, it is reputed that her youngest son, Theobald, became unnerved and sought refuge behind his mother's back. Supposedly, she "...publicly rebuked him, saying, 'Is it trying to hide behind my backside you are...the place you came from?'"[361]

The story is also told that the day after she gave birth at sea to one of her sons, her ship was attacked by Turkish pirates. When Grace heard the sounds of the struggle up on deck, she painfully arose from her birthing bed, grabbed a gun, and joined her crew in their struggle. Her appearance so inspired her somewhat demoralized crew that they quickly dispensed with the Turks.[362]

For many years Grace and her fleet of Irish galleys controlled the coast of western Ireland, forcing all those who wished to sail the coast to pay tribute to her and her loyal crewmembers. However, in her 56th year she was finally subdued by the brutal English Governor Richard Bingham, who had been sent by Queen Elizabeth to complete the subjugation of the Irish. He captured Grace, imprisoned her, and was planning to execute her after confiscating all of her lands and holdings. Just before her execution was scheduled to take place, Bingham unexpectedly pardoned her after obtaining her promise to abandon her buccaneering ways, but during this time he had reduced her to an impoverished state.[363]

In 1593 Bingham feared that Grace, though nearly penniless, might serve as a rallying point for the sense of rebellion that was growing throughout the land in response to his harsh rule on Elizabeth's behalf. To keep control over her, Bingham arrested her youngest son and her brother-in-law, Donal-na-Plopa.[364] In response, Grace wrote directly to Queen Elizabeth I, seeking both an audience and an alliance. When Elizabeth took too long to respond from Grace's perspective, she boldly sailed her galley to London and appeared at Court unexpectedly and uninvited. For some unknown reason, Elizabeth agreed to give her an audience. Perhaps it was a case of one strong woman fascinated by another -- a real rarity in those days. During her public appearance, Grace is said to have suddenly and loudly sneezed. One of the many court dandies offered her an exquisitely embroidered lace handkerchief. Grace seized the proffered handkerchief, loudly blew her nose, and then threw the handkerchief into the fireplace. The Court essentially gasped in unison and awaited Elizabeth's command of "off with her head", borrowing several centuries ahead from Alice in Wonderland. When Elizabeth finally responded, she admonished her guest for her offensive behavior. Specifically, she chided Grace for being rude, indicating that she had received a very fine gift and should have carefully folded it into her pocket. Grace replied by noting that apparently the Irish had much higher standards of personal hygiene than the English, since they wouldn't wear soiled items next to their bodies. At first the Court was stunned into silence. Then some members slowly began to respond with soft laughter until the entire Court was roaring. Elizabeth was obviously pleased, and quite taken with her uninvited guest.[365] A treaty of sorts was concluded, and Grace won the freedom of her son and brother-in-law. Unfortunately, at Bingham's intervention, her wealth was never restored.

Some say she died in poverty on Clare Island in 1603.[366] Others claim that she died as she had lived -- at sea. In any event, she will live forever in the hearts of the Irish, and not soon be forgotten by the "Bloody British" either.

Chapter Twenty-six: Anne Bonny, the Scourge of the Carolinas

*N*o one can study the buccaneers who ravaged the coastline of the Carolinas during the Golden Age of Piracy without being attracted to Anne Bonny and her notorious partner, Mary Read. These women rose to fame during an era when Pirate Rules dictated that no one could bring a female on board ship. In fact, any attempt to smuggle a woman on board in disguise was a crime punishable by death.

Anne Bonny was born out of wedlock in County Cork, Ireland, to William Cormac, a well-to-do lawyer, and his wife's maid, Peg Brennan. To escape his wife's ire upon the discovery of his indiscretion, he took Peg and their child to America where they settled in Charleston, South Carolina.[367] Cormac resumed his successful law career, and the family joined the socially prominent St. Paul's parish, according to surviving Church records from 1709.[368] William Cormac eventually became a large and wealthy Charleston landowner. His work was so demanding, though, that he was not able to give sufficient attention to his daughter's upbringing. After her mother's death when

Anne was only thirteen, the girl blossomed into a beautiful young lady with a porcelain white complexion and striking shoulder-length red hair, reflecting her Irish heritage.[369] She was also a strong-willed young woman with a definite mind of her own and a general disregard for the rules of Charleston society.[370] At the age of sixteen (or nineteen, depending upon which version of her history you believe),[371,372] she defied the plans her father had to marry her to a respected member of Charleston's upper class. Instead, she eloped with James Bonny, a common sailor she had recently met on the Charleston docks.[373] The couple soon fled to New Providence, Bahamas, a well-known gathering place for pirates in the Americas.

Once in New Providence, the couple's ardor began to cool rapidly. William Bonny became an informer on suspected pirates for the Governor, much to Anne's disgust. She, in turn, caught the eye and inflamed the passion of a local pirate called "Calico Jack" Rackham. Rackham, whose accomplishments as a pirate captain were modest at best, has remained known in the annals of piracy primarily because of his association with the fiery Anne Bonny. Eventually, Anne returned Rackham's feelings, and he became her first true love. Rackham offered a large sum of money to Anne's estranged husband to divorce her. Instead, William Bonny appealed to the Governor to have her publicly flogged based on the prescribed punishment for married women involved in an affair. Of course, there was no corresponding punishment for married men similarly involved.

The night before her punishment was to be publicly rendered, Rackham stole a local ship, and with a handpicked crew that obviously included Anne, fled to the open seas. To conceal her sex from the rest of the crew, Anne dressed as a man and strapped down her breasts under a rather loose-fitting blouse.[374]

Among their various early conquests on the open seas was a Dutch merchant ship. The crew of the Dutch merchantman offered little opposition to Rackham's pirates. The single exception was an Englishman who put up a stiff resistance to being captured, until offered a place among Rackham's men if he agreed to quit fighting. After his acquiescence, we have seen that that Bonny (Chapter Sixteen) formed an immediate and strong friendship with the new seaman, inflaming Rackham's jealously until Anne revealed that her new friend was another woman in disguise -- Mary Read.[375]

As Terrance Zepke[376] suggests, the question of whether or not Anne Bonny was initially interested in having an affair with her new companion was never nor can ever be addressed. Anne was certainly a women with a determined will and strong appetites. She tired readily of her first husband when he became an informer for the governor, and Rackham himself was certainly not the most daring of buccaneers.

Rackham and his crew continued their buccaneering activities for a brief period of time, but their pirate careers were drawing to an end. They returned to Jamaica in the early fall; and in November of 1720, their ship was attacked by a military vessel under the command of Captain Jonathan Barnet. Barnet had been commissioned by Governor Rodgers to pursue and capture those pirates in the area who particularly annoyed him. Rackham and all of his male crewmembers were still too drunk from a celebration the previous evening to put up a resistance and fled to the hold of their ship. Anne and Mary were left alone to offer a vigorous but eventually futile defense. Tradition claims that the two women divided their efforts between swearing at and firing on the British, and similarly cursing at and firing into the ship's hold at their male counterparts. The entire crew was captured, thrown in prison, and put on trial. At the trial the crew, both men and women, were found guilty and condemned to death.[377] However, Anne and Mary both pled their bellies, a legal term of the era indicating that they were pregnant.[378] So, their sentences were deferred until their pregnancies had run their courses. Anne's final meeting with Calico Jack was less than romantic. Apparently her last words to Rackham were: "If you had stayed and fought like a man, you need not be hanged like a dog."[379]

After that famous meeting, Anne Bonny's story becomes much more difficult to confirm. There appear to be no prison or legal records indicating that her sentence was ever executed.[380] However, rumors of her fate abound. Some say that her father used his influence and wealth to have her spirited back to Charleston, where she lived out her life in peace and obscurity. Sandra MacLean Clunies and Bruce Roberts propose a number of alternative theories:[381]

> Did she give birth on 21 April 1791 to an infant son, John, whose father was listed as Jack Rackham? Did she leave for South Carolina and then to Virginia where she married Joseph Burleigh and had eight more children? Or was her child fathered by a Dr. Michael Radcliffe [who may have been initially bribed by Anne's father to examine her in prison and attest to her pregnancy], whose life he had saved and who took Anne and the infant to Norfolk, Virginia, where they joined a party of pioneers headed westward?

As is so often the case with our Golden Age pirates, her full story will, in all likelihood, never be known. In any event, we are fairly certain that she never returned to her infamous life of piracy.

Chapter Twenty-seven: Mary Read: The Other Half of the Deadly Petticoat Duo

*U*ndocumented stories of Mary Read's early life suggest that she was born in poverty to a sailor (who subsequently was lost at sea) and his mentally unstable wife.[381] Her mother's first child and husband's only heir, a male, died in infancy. Perhaps as a result of an affair she had with another man, her second child, Mary, was born shortly thereafter. Throughout her early childhood, Mary's mother dressed her as a male in order to deceive and receive financial support from her deceased son's paternal grandmother.[382,383] As a teenager, presumably still disguised as a male, she worked on the docks in Plymouth, England. What followed next depends on which version of her legend one embraces.

In her usual male attire, she enlisted in the British army where she fell in love with a fellow soldier. Once he learned her true identity, he quickly returned her affections. She and her lover were both outstanding soldiers and very popular with the other men in the company. When they confessed the nature of their situation to their captain, he gave them honorable discharges from the service instead of exposing them to the usual punishment called for in army regulations.[384] They immediately married, with Mary wearing a dress for the first and probably only time in her life, and opened a tavern in Breda, Holland, called the Three Horseshoes.[385] While the tavern generated a good income for the couple during the remainder of Queen Anne's War, Mary's husband died suddenly of a fever near the end of hostilities. Furthermore, the signing of the peace treaty ending the war deprived the Three Horseshoes of many of its best customers, as most of the British officers in the area went back to England. Mary was forced to close the tavern and return to sea, eventually becoming a crewmember on the Dutch merchant ship that was ultimately captured by Calico Jack.

Whether or not there initially was any romantic attraction between Anne and Mary, the latter soon became intimately involved with another young English sailor by the name of Tom Deane.[386] Although Deane seems to have been very popular with the crew in general, one brutish (and certainly more skilled in arms) bully in the crew disliked him intensely, constantly taunting him and eventually forcing him into a duel. Mary recognized that her lover, whom she now regarded as her new husband, would be no match for his dueling opponent when they landed the next day. She accosted the bully in question and insulted him so extensively that he was forced to challenge her to a duel before confronting Tom Deane. Once the duel was begun the following day, Mary valiantly fought the more powerful male. He thrust at her but lost his balance. As he was recovering, she tore open her shirt and exposed herself to her opponent. While he momentarily paused to gape at her in surprise, she ran him through.[387]

Shortly after this confrontation, the lady pirates revealed their identities to the remainder of the crew, and they were readily accepted on an equal footing with their male companions.

As was indicated in the preceding chapter, Mary Read was apprehended with the rest of "Calico Jack's" crew, tried and found guilty of piracy, and sentenced to be executed. However, like Anne Bonny, she pled her belly and had her sentence postponed until she completed her pregnancy. Unfortunately she contracted fever and died in prison during April of 1721.[388]

Chapter Twenty-eight: Madame Cheng, Prostitute and Incredibly Successful Pirate Queen of the South China Sea

$\mathcal{M}$adame Cheng, Chang, Ching or Cheng I Sao began her career as a pirate in 1801 as the wife of the famous Korean buccaneer Ching Yih. Prior to her wedding, she was reputed to have been a prostitute. Although not as well known to Western pirate enthusiasts as Anne Bonny and Mary Read, she was certainly more successful in her chosen career.

Ching Yih, unlike his brothers and father, chose to avoid participating in the Vietnamese Civil War and, instead, elected to pursue life on the high seas of China as a pirate leader. Local seamen had been forced for years to attack Chinese and, occasionally, foreign merchant shipping to feed their starving families and themselves. However, their efforts were conducted on an individual and highly disorganized basis. Ching Yih recognized the tremendous opportunity presented by this situation and organized these necessity-driven pirates from along the Chinese coastline into a force with which to be reckoned.[389] By 1807 he had combined the pirate fleets into a large and growing confederation of over 600 pirate junks and 30,000 crewmen.[390]

In 1801 he made what may well have been the most important decision of his career: he chose to marry.[391] He assembled twenty female captives or slaves, and chose the one he found to be the most attractive, Cheng Yih Sao. In addition to being very beautiful, she apparently was also quite tall for that era. Ching Yih plied his intended bride with jewels and descriptions of the luxurious lifestyle that awaited her once she consented to his proposal. However, she would only agree to marry him after he promised to make her his partner and place one-third of his fleet under her command.

Ching Yih organized his pirates' federation into six separate fleets and designated each by a different color: red, blue, green, black, white, and yellow. Each fleet had a coastal base, and territory of operations over which they had exclusive control.[392] After their marriage, Madame Cheng had command of the red fleet and the area around Canton, which was her base.

Husband and wife proved to be invulnerable to attack from the Chinese emperor. Furthermore, they collected protection money from all ships operating in the South China Sea. They also paid local farmers along the coast to grow produce for their crews. Needless to say, the peasants along the Chinese coast gave their loyalty to the pirates and not to the emperor.

In 1708, at the peak of his career, Ching Yih suddenly disappeared at sea, probably washed overboard during a violent storm.[393] Madame Cheng eventually took over leadership of the entire federation. To consolidate her power, she married her adopted son.[394] who was also a fearsome pirate leader and a prominent member of the federation.[395]

Madame Cheng proved to be an accomplished organizer, skilled leader, and fearless warrior. She imposed a number of new restrictions on the federation and enforced them ruthlessly. For example, no crewman was allowed to marry without her permission. No crewmember was allowed to rape a captive woman or female villager, or even a woman who supposedly gave her consent to his advances. Nor was a pirate allowed to harm any of the local peasants who lived along the coast growing produce for the fleet. Enforcement of her edicts or punishment for those who violated them was always the same -- decapitation.[396] Moreover, unlike her first husband, Madame Cheng did not restrict her buccaneering activities to non-European victims.[397] The Emperor, who was unable to make any headway against Madame Cheng himself, reluctantly solicited western aid, specifically from the Americans and Portuguese, to bring her under his control. On November 19, 1809, the "foreign devils" and their royal Chinese allies surrounded and attacked her and her crew early in the morning while they were at anchor.[398] After a fierce battle lasting for several hours, Madame Cheng prevailed.

Finally realizing that a military victory was not an option, the Emperor turned to diplomacy. In 1810 the Emperor offered a general pardon to all members of the pirate federation and many took advantage of this generous offer. The remaining members of the various color fleets began to fall out among themselves. Realizing that the federation was beginning to crumble, Madame Cheng sued for peace for herself and her red fleet captains with the Emperor. Through her skillful negotiations, she secured a commission in the Imperial navy for her new husband, who then took on the job of pirate hunter, which he fulfilled with tremendous zeal and success. Madam Cheng maintained control of a massive smuggling operation and opened a brothel and gambling house, which she ran until her senior years. She died in 1844 most likely at the age of 59, depending on the source.[399,400] In spite of her overwhelming accomplishments, the author of "The Lady Was A Pirate" notes that she is largely ignored or assigned a minor role by Chinese historians,[401] who inappropriately give most or all of the credit for her achievements to her first husband, Ching Yih.

Chapter Twenty-nine: Rachel Wall, the First American-born Petticoat Pirate

$\mathcal{R}$achel Wall was born Rachel Schmidt on a farm outside of Carlisle, Pennsylvania, sometime in the late 1750s.[402] The date of her birth may well have rendered her the first petticoat pirate actually born in the United States. She was an attractive young girl by all reports, with beautiful blue eyes and long brown hair. She was raised in a devout Presbyterian home[403] and undoubtedly had a very proper upbringing. Unfortunately, farm life had little appeal for Rachel, and she secretly longed to put it behind her.

When she was approximately sixteen, an opportunity finally arose for her to abandon her life on the farm. After her grandfather, Joseph Kirsch,[404] died, Rachel and her mother attended the funeral in Harrisburg, Pennsylvania, which is located on the Susquehanna River. While in Harrisburg, she had her first opportunity to visit the water and docks, and immediately fell in love with her new environment. But, her affection was not restricted solely to the docks. She soon met a fisherman named George Wall, who had served as a privateer during the American Revolution. They quickly developed very strong feelings for each other and eloped to Boston. George returned to his life as a fisherman, and Rachel became a house servant. However, their life together was not to remain simple for long.

In her own words, Rachel[405] confessed that her husband "…tricked me into leaving my service and take me into bad company." The Walls and five other sailor acquaintances of George's developed a fresh and very effective wrinkle on the sweet trade. A friend of George's supposedly lent him a fishing schooner in return for a share of the gang's overall profits. During normal weather, they acted as ordinary fishermen, waiting for a severe storm to arise. When such a storm did occur, they would set the schooner adrift, making it appear to be a victim of the storm. When another ship approached, Rachel would stand on the deck waving and pleading to be rescued. If the vessel did attempt to come to her aid, Wall and his companions would immediately kill the would-be rescuers, steal all of their valuables, and sink their ship, making it appear to be a victim of the storm.[406]

Their scheme was quite successful for over a year. During that period, they seized a number of ships, killed several seamen, and made off with over $6,000 in cash and various other items of value, which was an impressive sum in those days.[407] Unfortunately, they underestimated the severity of one particular storm, and George and another crewman were washed overboard and lost.[408]

Ironically, the survivors were eventually rescued and returned to Boston. Rachel resumed her life as a household servant, but could never entirely forget her days of "easy pickins". What occurred next depends on which of the many colorful stories about her final days you choose to embrace.

One tale asserts that she began sneaking aboard docked vessels and stealing valuables while the crew slept. According to this version, she was eventually apprehended and put on trial.

A second version claims that she may have become a prostitute, soliciting sailors, then robbing them in their sleep. This version suggests that she may have killed a sailor, been apprehended, and put on trial.

Perhaps the most colorful version claims that Rachel was walking the streets of Boston when she saw a seventeen-year-old girl, Margaret Bender, who was wearing a lovely bonnet. Rachel was so taken with the bonnet that she supposedly tore it off Margaret's head and tried to rip out the girl's tongue.[409] Arrested by local police, she was soon put on trial. While she admitted to being a pirate, she denied having ever killed anyone. She was found guilty anyway, and on October 8, 1789, and was hanged.[410] Her last words were reportedly "...into the hands of the Almighty God I committ my soul, relying on his mercy...and die an unworthy member of the Presbyterian Church, in the 29th year of my age."[411]

Chapter Thirty: Sadie the Goat

$\mathcal{I}$ cannot think of any other tale like that of Sadie the Goat, which so clearly illustrates how far removed the real female buccaneers were from the alluring femme fatales of the silver screen. Some might even question Sadie's claim to being a petticoat pirate, since she and her crew sailed the New York and Hudson Rivers rather than any ocean. Nevertheless, she is one of my very favorites, and hers is a story certainly worthy of telling.

"Sadie the Goat" Farrell was eventually the leader of the Charlton Street Boys,[412] one of the many street gangs that terrorized the "Bloody" Fourth Ward of New York City during the middle of the nineteenth century. These gangs, often composed of immigrants united by religion, race, and/or country of origin, were immortalized in the thrilling movie "The Gangs of New York" starring Liam Nesson and Leonardo de Caprio. Some of the better known gangs were the Pug Uglies, the Dead Rabbits, the Whyos, the Patsy Conroys, Corcoran's Roosters, the Monk Eastman Gang, and the notorious Five Points Gang.[413]

Sadie and her original followers hung out in the basement of one of the most dangerous locations on Water Street -- the Hole-in-the-Wall tavern. A travel guide of the city called it "the most violent street in the continent", while another warned readers "absolutely to stay clear after dark."[414] The Water Street saloon was under the iron-fisted control of a notorious female bouncer, six-foot Gallus Mag,[415] whose usual attire featured a sap around her wrist as well as a pistol tucked into her waistband. She was particularly well known for blackjacking anyone who offended her, then dragging them out of the tavern by their ear held tightly between her undoubtedly filed and sharpened teeth. As a final punishment, she would often bite off the ear in question and store it in a pickling jar behind the bar.[416,417] Sadie unfortunately had a falling out with Mag on one occasion and ended up donating one of her ears to the infamous jarred collection.[418]

Sadie's nickname of "the Goat" was apparently based on her practice of head-butting an intended victim in the stomach and thereby disabling them.[419] Her male accomplice(s), following closely behind with her, would then rob the fallen victim. In 1869, following her run in with Gallus Meg, she, undoubtedly embarrassed, decided to move to a new area, turn to more profitable enterprises, and enlist a more aggressive gang.

Down on the docks she watched members of the Charlton Street Gang try but fail to seize a tied-up sloop. Under her proffered leadership, they boldly stole a sloop, hoisted their own Jolly Roger, and began raiding merchant ships and private homes along the Hudson and Harlem Rivers.[420] According to local newspapers of the day, Sadie and her crew kidnapped and held a number of wealthy Hudson Valley family members for ransom, including men, women, and children. She became overly enamored with her role as a pirate queen and supposedly ended the lives of several crewmembers that earned her displeasure, and perhaps even one or two well-known citizens of the Hudson Valley area, by having them "walk the plank".[421] The Hudson Valley farmers reacted by forming an armed vigilante group to stop her outrages and achieve some sort of retribution a few months after Sadie launched her pirate career. As a result, Sadie and the survivors of her gang were forced to abandon piracy and return to the less profitable street crimes as a livelihood.

It is reported that shortly before the police finally shut down The Hole-in-the-Wall tavern, Sadie and a much-mellowed Gallus Mag renewed their friendship. As a tribute to this restored friendship, Mag supposedly returned Sadie's pickled ear to her,[422] which Sadie is said to have worn in a locket around her neck for the rest of her criminal career.[423]

Chapter Thirty-one: Gunpowder Gertie and the *Tyrant Queen*

$\mathcal{C}$athy Converse[424] is the author of an excellent review of the petticoat pirates entitled "The Lady Was A Pirate". One of the most intriguing female buccaneers featured in her work is Imogene Stubbs, more commonly known as Gunpowder Gertie. According to Converse, Gertie is one of the last female buccaneers to ply her craft prior to the onset of the modern area.

Imogene was born in Whitby, England, in 1879 and immigrated to Sandon, British Columbia, when she was approximately sixteen. Shortly after her family's arrival, her mother, Violet, was killed when their home was destroyed by avalanche and her father, George, turned to the bottle for solace.[425] As a result, Imogene was essentially left on her own to survive solely by her wits and ambition. Realizing that there was no way a single woman, let alone a young girl, could get ahead in her male-dominated society, Imogene cut her hair, disguised herself as man and assumed a male personality. It was a role to which she apparently adapted readily. She had a strong mechanical aptitude in general, and was extremely gifted in dealing with steam engines in particular. She began as a coal hand on a paddle wheeler, and rapidly rose to the position of mechanic until it was discovered that she was, in fact, a woman. The accidental discovery led to her immediate discharge since, in spite of her obvious skill, she was deemed unfit to work in a man's world.[426]

Imogene was initially infuriated, but soon vowed to concentrate her reaction to extracting revenge upon those who had dismissed her so cavalierly. From 1898 until 1903, she terrorized the Kootenay River system of British Columbia, focusing exclusively on the steam ships earning their livelihoods in that area.[427] She boldly launched her new pirate career by stealing a police gunboat from the railroad line on which it was being transported. The stolen gunboat *Witch* was renamed the *Tyrant Queen* by Imogene, or "Gunpowder Gertie" as she was soon to be known. The *Tyrant Queen* was capable of a top speed of 22 knots, rendering her the fastest steamship of her time. Furthermore, she had been retrofitted with ducted propellers, which gave her a particularly shallow draft, perfect for moving rapidly among the estuaries and coves that lined the Kootenay River system.[428]

Gunpowder Gurtie and her pirate crew would seemingly appear out of thin air to take control of a commercial steamship, the object of her wrath and her sole target. After boarding their intended victim, she and her crew would seize any gold or silver bullion that the steamship was transporting from one or more of the local mines, and any mine payroll that might be on board. As the coup de grace, they would line up all the ship's passengers and relieve them of their valuables at gunpoint.[429] No one dared defy her for she was as skilled with a Gatling gun as she was with a steam engine.

Eventually, a male member of her own crew, Bill Henson, betrayed Imogene because of his dissatisfaction over his share of the seized treasure. She was apprehended, tried, convicted, and sentenced to life in prison. However, she was not destined to spend many years in prison, for she contracted and died of pneumonia in 1912 without ever revealing the hiding place of her seized treasure.[430]

The story of her life makes her the very embodiment of the classic female pirate, eluding authorities throughout her five-year career. However, that is far from the end of her story.

Imogene Stubbs or Gunpowder Gertie was actually an extremely complex April Fool's Day hoax, perpetrated by the well-known Canadian story teller, Carolyn McTaggart.[431] Ms. McTaggart's tale, which originally appeared in the local newspaper, the *Kootenay Review*, is basically reported above. In spite of this apparent hoax, Gunpowder Gertie had so captured the public's imagination that her tale is still widely accepted as actual fact to this very day.

Many continue to regard Gunpowder Gertie as a real person in spite of the author's own denial:[432]

> "The truth is, Gertie only exists as a figment of my overactive imagination. I made her up to explain a treasure hunt for some schoolchildren I was working with and in order to make her more credible, added a lot of the local history I've grown to love. We used her to take a tour of the area learning local history (true stuff as well) and then dug up one of her treasures at the beach before we told them the truth. It was when the parents believed it (guess what, we had a lady pirate on Kootenay Lake in 1898 and everyone just forgot!), that it seemed too good not to have a little fun with it. A local paper, The *Kootenay Review*, ran the story as an April Fool's joke along with the explanation of how she'd been "lost" to history. It was amazing how many people fell for it hook, line and sinker! Best joke I've ever played and to my knowledge nobody got hurt (ok, disappointed, maybe) -end of story- I thought. Then, a few years later, Gertie turned up on her own, somehow, the story got sent to the CBC -not me, honest- and was used in a segment of Bob Johnson's program, *This Day in History* and they thought it was a true story. And that's how I ended up becoming an historical storyteller. I have much more of her life written out, and several adventures that I can tell, as well as the

original legend, and have told her story as far as the Yukon
International Storytelling Festival and England. She's taken on a life
of her own. The *Tyrant Queen* has floated down Baker St. in the local
parade, I have a treasure chest with treasure, there was a traveling
exhibit of "artifacts and fiction". There's even a mockumentary of her
life available on video. It's been lots of fun and ten years later, I still
run into people who think she was real. And now, in a twisted way,
she is real local history. When my father built my treasure chest when
I was 5, I don't think he imagined I'd still be playing with it when I
turned 40!

Carolyn McTaggart"

PART III:
THE PIRATE CHASERS

*M*erchant sea trading attracted pirates almost from its inception. In turn, the pirates had barely set sail before the pirate chasers or catchers pursued them. This latter group of individuals, who were every bit as interesting as the pirates they hunted, seemed to fall into three main categories.

The first category contained seamen who were originally recruited to track pirates wanted by various legal authorities. Many of these individuals ended up as more famous buccaneers than those whom they were originally hired to pursue. One of the most interesting pirate catchers in this category was Captain William Kidd, who was originally commissioned by King George III to bring a list of notorious pirates to justice. Uppermost on this list was the dashing William Tew, who had already been slain before the signing of the commission. (Tew's and Kidd's stories are recounted in Chapters Five and Seven, respectively.)

The second category of pirate catchers was composed of one-time pirates who had reformed for a variety of reasons and now pursued their former brethren. One of the better-known members of this category was the intriguing William Hornigold, who is credited with formally introducing piracy into the Bahamas. He was also the tutor of many famous future buccaneers, including Edward Teach or Blackbeard. However, he retired from piracy, was granted a royal pardon by Woodes Rogers, and eagerly embraced the role of pirate catcher after receiving his pardon.

The last category of pirate chasers is perhaps the largest, including both career military men and government officials who were determined to render the area in which they presided safe for normal citizens. One of the most famous members of this group was Julius Caesar, himself a captive of pirates.

Chapter Thirty-two: Julius Caesar, Pirate Captive and Pirate Chaser

*U*ndoubtedly, every reader of this collection of tales can think of at least one of Julius Caesar's many titles -- Conqueror of Gaul, Member of the Triumvirate (during the last days of the Roman Republic), First Consul of Rome, Dictator of Rome, Dictator in Perpetuity, Roman Deity (two years after his assassination), or lover of Cleopatra, who gave birth to his only son, Caesarian. But, how many of you would have suggested pirate hostage or successful pirate chaser?

Pirates had existed in the Mediterranean area throughout history. However, the influence and power of the Cilician pirates, who occupied much of modern western Turkey, increased significantly during the last two centuries BC. This growth was aided by the Roman upper class, including the Senators, who were often willing to overlook their activities. The pirates, in turn, supplied many of the slaves needed to maintain the estates of these same members of the Roman upper class. Moreover, the Cilician pirates seemed to initially avoid armed conflict with Romans on either land or sea. Yet as their power and numbers grew, so did their inclination to confront the Romans directly.[433,434]

In 75 BC, Caesar was journeying to Greece to study, when Cilician pirates seized his ship.[435] When the pirates initially sought the standard ransom of 25 talents, Caesar, an aspiring statesman, was indignant and demanded that the ransom requested be no less than 50 talents[436] of silver, as befitted a man of his status. While the Cilicians readily and laughingly complied with Caesar's demands, the raising of such a large sum required that Caesar remain their hostage for thirty-eight days. He passed away the time by joining the Cilicians in their athletic games, composing poetry, and giving speeches as well as readings of his work to his captors. Whenever they did not show sufficient appreciation for his efforts, Caesar presumably chided them for their stupidity and assured them that once he was freed, he would return, capture them, and have them all crucified. The pirates assumed this was in jest, and found him to be quite amusing. Once he was released, however, Caesar sailed away, assembled a small, armed fleet, and returned to the island where he had been held captive. His forces quickly overcame the pirates and again, as he had forewarned, he seized his ransom, anything else they had of value, and had all of the pirates crucified. As a show of compassion for the kind manner in which he had been held during his imprisonment, Caesar is rumored to have had all 500 of the pirates' throats slit or legs broken prior to their execution to diminish the pain of the actual crucifixion.

Chapter Thirty-three: Pompey the Great, Perhaps the Ultimate Pirate Chaser

naeus Pompeius Magnus, or Pompey the Great, was a noted Roman politician and military commander. He may be best remembered as a member of the unofficial alliance known as the First Triumvirate.   This Triumvirate, which also included Julius Caesar and Marcus Licinius Cassius, ruled Rome during the last years of the Roman Republic.

Pompey eventually became jealous of Caesar's impressive military victories in Gaul and his closeness to Cassius. Since he remained in Rome itself throughout this period, he had the opportunity to form a bond with some of the more conservative members of the Senate, who distrusted Caesar's every growing popularity with the citizens of Rome.   Ultimately, these political maneuverings led Caesar to cross the Rubican in 49 BC, and to initiate the Roman Civil War, which proved to be Pompey's downfall.[437] Nevertheless, a reasonable case can be made for regarding him as the greatest pirate chaser of all time.

As was discussed in the preceding chapter, the Cilician pirates were becoming a real threat to the supremacy of the Roman state by the last century BC.   In 101 BC the Roman Senate passed its first anti-piracy law, which effectively closed Rome's Asian harbors to the Cilicians.[438] Matters continued to deteriorate, however; and by 67 BC, the Cilicians threatened to cut off the Romans from their Mediterranean-based food supply and starve the empire into submission.[439]   The dire nature of this threat prompted the Senate to give Pompey extraordinary powers to rid the area of pirates under a new anti-piracy law, *lex Gabinia de Piratis persequendis.*[440]   Lex Gabinia put Pompey in command of 500 warships, 120,000 infantry, 5,000 cavalry, and 24 legates or deputy commanders. He also received total authority over the area from the coast inland for up to 50 miles, and a budget of over 6,000 talents.[441,442]

Pompey began by dividing the Mediterranean up into thirteen districts with each under the command of a separate legate. Acting simultaneously within their districts, each legate had his troops seek out Cilician strongholds and small, hidden fleets. He then ordered the legates to destroy them, capturing or killing those who offered resistance. Key to the overall strategy, Pompey commanded the reserve naval fleet, and swept the few Cilician ships that initially escaped from their individual districts back into the arms of the waiting legate fleets. Pompey also had the foresight to allow captured Cilicians to join with their families and be relocated away from the coast of modern southern Turkey. Up to [443] 10,000 pirates may have been killed or executed during the three-month campaign.

While some feel that Pompey's claims are exaggerated, and that the contributions of others were minimized, it still was an amazing feat. Even if one takes into account the claims that the Cilicians, who were members of a defined nation, were significantly different from the pirates of the early eighteenth century, it still seems difficult to deny Pompey the Great the title of the most effective pirate chaser of all time.

Chapter Thirty-four: Woodes Rogers, the Greatest Pirate Chaser of the Golden Age

*A*s a young man growing up in Poole on England's southern coast and later in the seaport town of Bristol, Woodes Rogers gave little indication that he would be the most effective buccaneer chaser of the Golden Age of Piracy. He would contribute more to its eventual collapse than any other single individual of his era.

He was born into a seafaring family. His father was a merchant and ship owner, with part of his fleet invested in privateers focusing primarily on French shipping, and Woodes followed enthusiastically in his footsteps.[444] Rogers married Sarah Whetstone, the daughter of Admiral Sir William Whetstone, which significantly enhanced his social standing and financial security. He quickly became a Merchant Venturer and Freeman of the City.[445]

Rogers took over control of his father's business at the same time. He prospered initially, but suffered with his fellow merchants as a result of various factors such as the growing harassment of British shipping by pirates and, at least in Rogers' case, poor money management skills. In 1708 he was placed in charge of a locally sponsored privateering mission focused on Spanish and French interests along the Pacific Coast. William Dampier agreed to serve as his navigator. Woodes was issued a Letter of Marque and given command of two 36-gun warships: the 350-ton *Duke* and the 260-ton *Duchess* with a combined crew of 333 men.[446]

The two warships rounded Cape Horn in January-February of 1709,[447] staying away from land as much as possible to avoid detection, and proceding on to the West Coast where the Spanish would least expect them. They captured several Spanish treasure galleons, held at least one Spanish town ransom, and accumulated a treasure in precious metals, jewels, and fine silks estimated to be worth 4 million dollars on the Indian market of the day.[448]

In addition, when they anchored off the presumably deserted island of Juan Fernandez, 400 miles west of Valparaiso, Chile,[449] they discovered a Scottish seaman named Alexander Selkirk,[450] who had been abandoned there four years earlier at his own request. The *Duke* and *Duchess* returned to Bristol, England, in October of 1711 after having circumnavigated the world.[451]

A year after his return, Woods published a full account of his voyage entitled[452] "*A Cruising Voyage Round the World: First to the South Seas, Thence to the East Indies, and Homeward by the Cape of Good Hope...Containing A*

Journal of All the Remarkable Transactions…An Account of Alexander Selkirk's Living Alone Four Years and Four Months on an Island."

Two members of Rogers' prominent circle of friends seem to have been clearly inspired by the account. Daniel Defoe's *Robinson Crusoe* is certainly modeled after Alexander Selkirk. Furthermore, the lead character of Jonathan Swift's *Gulliver's Travels*, Gulliver himself, seems to be a composite of Dampier, Rogers, and Selkirk.[453]

One of the most interesting aspects of Woodes Rogers' voyage was the tremendous hue-and-cry that arose around Rodgers' captured booty and its disposition. First, the ever-greedy East India Company demanded that all of the booty be immediately given or turned over to them because of their trade monopoly in the area where Rogers' plundering occurred.[454] Next, there was a real threat that the British navy would impress Rogers' crew before Woodes could liberate the funds to pay them their overdue wages. It took over three years and an appeal to the House of Lords before the matter was finally resolved.[455] As for Woods Rogers himself, it is not clear exactly how much or when he received his share of the booty, but it was clearly a fortune. Yet, he was so successful in mismanaging the funds that he was forced to declare bankruptcy.

Woodes Rodgers was reduced to operating a slaver until 1717 when the British government appointed him the first Royal Governor of the new colony of the Bahamas.[456] His appointment was definitely not a political plum, however, since his primary if not sole responsibility was to clean up the pirate-infested area -- over 2,000 pirates are estimated to have lived there during this era -- and made it safe for respectable citizens again.

Woodes' first official act was a display of leniency: he offered a full pardon to all those who renounced piracy as a way of life. So when he arrived in the Bahamas with his small naval escort, he was heartily cheered like a conquering Roman hero by over 600 minor pirates anxious to accept his generous, one-time pardon. On the other hand, most of the notorious pirates, like William Teach or Blackbeard, who were dwelling in the Bahamas at the time, decided that the good old days were finally over and departed to seek a new, safer haven for their nefarious operations. The one defiant exception was Charles Vane, whose story was recounted in Chapter Ten.

Knowing that his small British escort squadron would soon depart and not so naive as to rely on the good will that his pardons had temporarily engendered, Woodes formed an organizing council made up of stalwart citizens of the island and members of his own party. When the British fleet did depart, a number of reformed ex-pirates did backslide into their former careers. However, a mass hanging in December of 1718[457] of recidivists gave pause to all of the others and firmly re-established Woodes' control over the Bahamas. Some of the ex-pirates even proved to be valuable resources in defending the Island from Spanish attack. Unfortunately, the British government essentially washed its hands of Rogers' obvious success in subduing the pirates and forced him and his companions to shoulder the entire expense of their efforts.

So, near the end of his first term as Royal Governor, he had to return to Britain with the threat of debtor's prison again hanging over his head. The British government finally came to its senses and agreed to pay him an adequate salary so that he could return to the Bahamas and begin his second term in 1729, with piracy essentially banished from the land. He died under mysterious circumstances in 1732 in his adopted home, possibly poisoned by one of the many enemies that his fair but stern rule had made.[458]

Chapter Thirty-five: Thomas Jefferson and the Barbary Pirates

*A*merica's current conflict with Al-Qaeda and other Muslim terrorists is far from the first time that we have struggled against such a cruel and unorthodox foe. At the very inception of our infant nation we were similarly involved with those who could be regarded as their historical antecedents, the Barbary pirates. These relentless pirates came from the Barbary Coast made up of the North African states of Tripoli, Tunis, Morocco, and Algiers.[459]

These states demanded an annual tributary payment, which was essentially protection money, from the various European powers that traded in their home waters, as well as an enormous ransom for any individual seaman and/or ships that fell into their grasps. Prior to and during the era of the American Revolution, the United States was first under the protection of the British and then the French and, therefore, immune from such payments. However, once we had secured our independence (1783), the Barbary rulers expected such payments from us as well.

In 1784 Congress decided to pay the customary tribute of $80,000[460] a year to the rulers of the Barbary Coast and instructed our representatives at the Court of France, Thomas Jefferson and John Adams, to begin negotiations with these same rulers. The situation escalated considerably the following year when Barbary pirates captured two American ships and their combined crews of 21 seaman, demanding $60,000 apiece for the release of each of the crewmen.[461]

Thomas Jefferson was adamantly opposed to the paying of any tribute to the Barbary States. He attempted to form an international coalition to confront the Barbary pirates, and the majority of the minor European powers involved were in agreement with his plans. Ultimately however, uncertainty about the action(s) to be pursued by Britain and France led to a collapse of the proposal.[462]

According to Gerald Gawalt,[463] Jefferson wrote to Ezra Stiles, the President of Yale College on December 26, 1786, to say that in regards to the American citizenry: "…it will be more easy to raise ships and men to fight these pirates into reason, than money to bribe them."

When Thomas Jefferson was elected President in 1801 and first assumed office, he refused to pay any further ransom or tribute to Tripoli. In response, the pasha of Tripoli declared war on the United States.[464] Despite a great deal of political opposition, Jefferson's own response was immediate: he sent a small fleet of naval frigates to the Mediterranean. Commodore Edward Preble aggressively pursued the war, and his actions in 1803-1804 caused Morocco to withdraw from the struggle. His five separate bombardments of

Tripoli also dampened much of the pasha's enthusiasm for the war that he had initiated. In the following year, Captain William Eaton, in charge of an American land force, threatened to invade Tripoli and depose the pasha, thereby forcing him to accept a treaty to bring hostilities to an end.[465] Since the negotiated agreement still required the United States to pay $60,000 for each of the captured sailors, the Senate refused to sign off on the treaty for over a year.

While the preamble to and the War of 1812 distracted the attention of the United States for a number of years, the situation was finally and fully resolved in 1815 when a Second Barbary War was waged.[466] In this engagement, the main American protagonist was Commodore Stephen Decatur. Decatur was the youngest seaman ever to attain the rank of captain in the American Navy. He had conducted himself with distinction during the First Barbary War, capturing the enemy ketch *Mastico*, rechristening her the *Intrepid*, then employing her in a night raid on Tripoli harbor where he destroyed the captured U.S. frigate *Philadelphia*. It is reported that the famous Lord Nelson is said to have deemed the raid "…the most daring act of the age."[467] While this endorsement has never been fully substantiated, Decatur immediately became the newest American naval hero and the first to not have seen action in the Revolutionary War.

At the outbreak of the Second Barbary War, Decatur sailed a squadron of 9-10 warships to the Mediterranean to finally resolve the tribute issue and to secure the release of American captives in Algiers. Within 48 hours his gunboat diplomacy had achieved his objectives and resulted in a new treaty incorporating all of the American demands.[468] From Algiers, Decatur next went to Tunis and Tripoli to seek the return of proceeds withheld by these governments and due to the United States during the War of 1812.[469] Again, Decatur met with immediate acquiescence and returned home as the "Conqueror of the Barbary Pirates".[470]

Like too many other American heroes, such as Alexander Hamilton, Decatur met his end not in service to his country but as a result of a personal tragedy. He was killed in a duel in which he only intended to wound his attacker, a fellow naval officer who had been found guilty of dereliction of duty at a court martial in which Stephen Decatur participated. As a result of the verdict, the officer in question was suspended from active service for a period of five years.[471] Again, like Alexander Hamilton before him, Decatur was shot in the stomach and took two days to die a very painful death.

An interesting footnote with which to end this tale is to recount a famous after-dinner toast that Decatur, as the Naval Commissioner (1816-1820), always used to close his formal gatherings: "Our Country! In her intercourse with foreign nations may she always be right, but right or wrong, our country!"[472] This toast is often misquoted as "My country, right or wrong!" and then erroneously cited as an example of American jingoism.

Chapter Thirty-six: Modern Pirate Chasers

*J*t is difficult to know exactly how to write the conclusion to a story that really has no end. Much of this volume has focused on individual pirates from the late sixteen hundreds to the middle eighteen hundreds, and so much has changed since those days. First of all, the action has shifted primarily from the Carolinas and the eastern coast of the United States, the Bahamas, and the Mediterranean to the Middle and Far East, and the East African coast. Next, the central characters of the current pirate tales are not strong, forceful leaders of men frequently glorified or glamorized by cults of personality. Instead, they are often faceless thanks to the use of ski masks and to the extent that they can be, identity-less. According to the August, 2007 edition of the *Smithsonian*, today's pirates range from the usual greedy cutthroats and thieves who reside along the coast to members of international criminal cartels. Gone are the days when pirates were individuals, wanting to live life on their own terms a la Terrance Zepke to individuals who just want to live -- and live as profitably as possible. Although no pirate is to be admired in the final sense, today's pirates seem to represent the very bottom of the human gene pool.

That's not to say that buccaneering isn't a profitable enterprise to this very day. According to the *Smithsonian*[473] and the U.S. Maritime Administration, approximately 95% of the world's trade travels on water, which in 2007, accounted for roughly six trillion dollars. That's big business from anybody's perspective. While the number of pirate raids is down from the heydays of the Golden Age, they are still far from insignificant. For example, in 2006, 239 major pirate attacks were reported, with cost estimates running into the billions of dollars.[474] Furthermore, it has been suggested that these estimates are probably under-reported by 50%.[475] Ship owners may well pressure their captains not to report successful pirate attacks in order to avoid both the associated bad publicity and the potential of their ships being inactively docked for months during any ensuing trial.

Finally, the pirate techniques and weapons of today also differ greatly from those of the Golden Age. Today's large merchantmen, ocean liners, cruise ships, and oil transports all have decks that are several stories above the water level. Since the pirates cannot merely swarm onto the victim's deck from their own ships as in days of old, they often attack with two or three high-powered dinghies and use megaphones and/or grenade-launchers to attract the attention of the commercial vessel's captain. Should the captain of the intended victim give in to their demands to stop in order to avoid the potential destruction of his ship, the pirates will rapidly mount their prize through the use of ropes and grappling hooks. Any of a number of possible outcomes might then ensue.

If the primary motivation of the attack is simple robbery, then the crew and any potential passengers will be stripped of all valuables. In addition, anything of worth that is readily portable onboard ship is also likely to be taken. All booty will quickly be removed to the dinghies and disappear. If the victim is an oil tanker, then it may be forced to sail to a designated meeting place where the precious cargo will be transferred to a waiting pirate tanker. Or, the target may be the actual ship itself, which may be taken to some hidden inlet, repainted and renamed, issued false papers, and sold on the open market. In these latter two instances, the crew's lives may well be in imminent peril. On the other hand, the main and growing purpose underlying the attack may be solely to hold the crew or the crew and ship for ransom.

A story from the *Smithsonian*[476] serves to illustrate graphically the similarities between current Muslim terrorists and the vicious modern-day pirates. One Korean and twelve Chinese pirates hijacked the Hong Kong registered merchantman the *Cheung Son* off the Chinese Coast in 1998. They bound and blindfolded the 23 crewmembers, beat them to death with clubs, and threw their bodies overboard. They then resold the vessel on the open market for $300,000.[477] Once Chinese authorities apprehended them, they were tried for piracy and murder, convicted, and sentenced to death by firing squad. They supposedly marched in chains to their deaths, defiantly singing a popular Ricky Martin song of the day. After their executions, their families were charged for the costs of each bullet used by the firing squad. This brief sketch of the modern pirates should convince the reader that they are every bit as brutal as their predecessors from the Golden Age. But what about those who pursue them?

During the Golden Age of Piracy and shortly thereafter, strong leaders like Governor Woodes Rogers of the Bahamas (Chapter 34), Governor Alexander Spotswood of Virginia, Blackbeard's ultimate nemesis, and President Thomas Jefferson of the United States (Chapter 35) spearheaded the struggle to bring the plague of piracy to an end. Now, in the modern information-communication age, the pursuit is much more organized on an international level.

In 1992 the International Maritime Bureau established the Piracy Reporting Center in Kuala Lumpur, which records hundreds of pirate attacks worldwide each year.[478] At present, the most dangerous area of all appears to be the waters around Somalia, such as the Gulf of Aden. Unfortunately, trying to avoid the area can add at least two weeks shipping time and several millions of dollars in extra fuel costs to the overall shipping expense. Nevertheless, two of the world's major shipping lines have now officially resorted to this very expensive alternative.[479]

The sooner a victimized vessel can contact the Center and provide the details of their attack and attackers, the sooner the Center can contact the warship nearest to the attack and initiate pursuit of the pirates. The obvious goal is to apprehend the pirates before they can reach the safety of the territorial waters of nations openly or tacitly in support of piracy.

The current head of the Piracy Reporting Center is Captain Noel Choong,[480] who is forced to maintain a certain aura of secrecy about himself and his actions for security reasons. He has been the recipient of numerous death threats. Captain Choong takes a very active role in the investigation and recovery of stolen ships along with his other duties. He is often forced to travel to various unsavory parts of the Middle East, Far East, and Africa, where he may act as the intermediary between pirates who have stolen a ship or corrupt government officials and the ship owners. The average going rate to reacquire a large stolen ship is $800,000,[481] and through careful and dangerous negotiation he is often able to return the ship to its rightful owners for a fraction of that price. In fact, he has established a standard reward of $50,000 for any informant who is willing to tell him where a stolen ship is hidden. Through his efforts and those of his fellow workers, the recent rate of pirate attacks has been nearly cut in half. According to the *Smithsonian*,[482] Choong has been quoted as saying: "We'll never see the end of piracy, just as we'll never see the end of robbery on land. But we're doing everything we can."

Now, just as I conclude this collection of tales, piracy is in the news[483] again. Somali pirates are becoming more and more daring, emphasizing their latest theme of ransom. **TIMES**ONLINE has reported that Somali pirates seized nine international ships in a period of just twelve days in November of 2008.[484] The most impressive of these was a super tanker, the *Sirius Star*, carrying a cargo of $100,000,000 worth of crude oil. Interestingly, the pirates did not attempt to sell the crude oil but, instead, tried to ransom the ship, cargo, and crew for $10,000,000.

Not all has gone the pirates' way during this period, though. Using one of their mother ships to extend their range of operations, the pirates brazenly challenged an Indian frigate, the *Tabar*, which handily destroyed the mother ship in the ensuing battle.

Since the onset of 2009, Somali pirates or terrorists have staged more than 66 attacks against international shipping. One of the most recent and certainly most alarming attacks to the United States was the temporary seizure of an American-flagged vessel for the first time in over 200 years. The merchantman was the *Maersk Alabama,* which was bound for malnourished Uganda and Somalia with food from USAID and other charitable agencies. Richard Phillips, the captain of the *Maersk Alabama,* ordered his unarmed crew of 19 into a secured stateroom and offered himself as a hostage to the pirates in place of the crew. As the weaponless crew freed themselves and began to counterattack the pirates, the latter fled the American-flagged vessel with the captive captain in one of the ship's canopy-covered lifeboats. Shortly afterward, the destroyer *USS Bainbridge* arrived on the scene. When the lifeboat ran out of fuel, it was eventually taken under tow by the *Bainbridge.* After a four-day standoff, during which Captain Phillips made a daring but unsuccessful attempt at escape, Navy seal sharpshooters assassinated the three remaining terrorists (one had surrendered earlier in the day) with single shots to the head. Thus, the United States demonstrated to these despicable terrorists the dangers encountered by challenging the world's greatest super power.

Given the vastness of space involved and the ability of the pirates to quickly move their base of operations, it seems that some sort of preemptive and permanent internationally based military action needs to be taken. If other nations are not willing to cooperate in such an important venture, however, we should never forget the lessons learned in the two Barbary Wars and the toast of Stephen Decatur.

GLOSSARY

A

ancient...another name for a (war) ensign or battle flag.

B

Barbary pirates...pirates from the North African states of Algiers, Morocco, Tunis, and Tripoli.

belaying pin...short, removable pin fitted into a ship's railing to which ropes used for navigation can be attached.

blunderbuss...a short gun or musket, often with a bell-shaped or flaring muzzle, used in confined quarters for impact rather than accuracy.

boarding hook...See grappling hook.

boatswain...according to Webster, a boatswain is "a petty officer... having immediate supervision of the deck force, of boat crews, and work parties engaged in maintenance of the hull, anchors, [life]boats and related equipment."

booty...anything of value taken by pirates from the victims, ships or settlements that they plundered.

Brethren of the Coast...an organization of privateers, active primarily in the Carribbean during the 1700s and 1800s, usually of Protestant origin, and often targeting French and Spanish Catholic seagoing interests.

brigantine or brig...according to Webster, "a two-masted square rigged vessel."

buccaneer...a French derived term based on a word for the wooden frame on which French backwoodsmen living in Hispaniola (modern Haiti and the Dominican Republic) barbecued or smoked their meat, such as sea cows. They had a deep hatred for the Spanish, who regarded them as fugitives, and often preyed upon Spanish shipping. By the seventeen hundreds the term had been broadened to include primarily French and English raiders who attacked

Spanish shipping all along the Spanish Main. Sometimes used generally to denote a pirate.

C

Cape Fear Region of coastal North Carolina…an area of southeastern North Carolina that includes Wilmington and a significant portion of the Cape Fear River.

Charles Johnson…the disputed but often presumed author of the "General Book of Pirates" (short title), which was first published on May 4, 1724.

Chevalier…a low ranking member of French nobility.

conscripted…forced into compulsory service, as in the military.

cutlass…a short sword with a thin, slightly curved blade, often featuring a hand guard attached to the hilt.

D

Ducat…various gold coins used in a number of European countries in the 1600 and 1700s.

E

East India Company…an English company chartered in 1600 by Queen Elizabeth I to trade with the new British colonies in India and Southeastern Asia.

F

first mate…a ship's officer who ranked second in command only to the captain. See definition of Quartermaster.

G

Golden Age of Piracy…the period from 1690 to 1730 that marked the heyday of piracy as a result of a pronounced increase in trade among Europe, the

United States, and the Bahamas. The peak in this period occurred with the cessation of Queen Anne's War in 1713, when 35,000 sailors and privateers were unemployed.

grappling line…a small anchor with three or more hooks fastened to the end of a rope used to hold an opponent's ship immobile during an attack.

I

impress…to conscript men for duty on a naval or pirate ship.

Indian Grand Mogul…according to Webster, "the sovereign of the empire founded in Hindustan by the Mongols under Baber in the sixteenth century".

J

Jolly Roger…a name applied to pirate flags or ensigns of the Golden Age. It is generally thought to be based sarcastically on the French term "jolie rouge" or pretty red. Others suggest that it may be based on the English term "Old Roger", a nickname for the Devil..

junk…a Chinese sailing vessel.

K

King William's War…the first portion of the French and Indian Wars (1689-1697), which was fought in Canada and New England between the French, the British and their respective Indian allies.

L

Letter of Marque…a contract originally written between the monarch of a country and a specific privateer, certifying that the privateer was officially acting on behalf of the monarch. Among other conditions, the terms of the Letter identified exactly whom the privateer could attack in the monarch's name.

Libertatia…"Republic of the Seas", which, according to Charles Johnson, was the name given to a democratically run pirate colony on the coast of Madagascar in the 1700s.

logwood…according **to** Webster it is a tree of Central America and the West Indies with a very hard brown heartwood or core used to make a dye.

Lord Protector…the ruler of the Kingdom of England, Scotland, Wales, and Ireland from 1655 to 1659.

M

Man-of-war…according to Webster, a ship of the line, warship, or armed naval vessel

merchantman…a cargo vessel with or without armament.

mizzen…the aft or rear mast on a sailing vessel.

N

no quarter…no mercy, i.e., all surviving opponents would supposedly be put to death

P

(golden) peso…the new gold piece or 8 reale of 1732, that was equivalent to the old piece-of-eight or Spanish dollar.

pieces-of-eight…an old Spanish peso that had a face value of eight reales.

Pirate…one who attacks on the sea (or occasionally on land), acts outside the law, and has no allegiance to any ruler or country.

Pirate Code…a general written statement, often used interchangeably with the term pirate contract, that defined conduct or behavior while on board ship, and punishments if any, that would be incurred by crewmen who violated the specified behavior.

pirate contract... an agreement on terms of employment between a pirate and his captain.

Prayer Book Rebellion...a revolt primarily in Cornwall and Devon by those remaining loyal to the Roman Catholic Church against Henry VIII's introduction of the Reformation-based Common Book of Prayer.

privateer...an individual who operated under a Letter of Marque from the monarch (later the Colonial Governor) of a given country that specified which enemy's ships he could attack as well as other conditions to which he must conform in order to claim to be acting on the monarch's behalf.

Q

Quartermaster...a petty officer responsible for the steering of a ship. According to some authors, the officer who was elected by the crew and ranked second in command to the ship's captain. He usually lead he the attack or boarding of an enemy or victim's ship.

Queen Anne's War...England and her colonies' name for the War of Spanish Succession.

R

reale...eight reales was a silver one ounce coin also known as the Spanish dollar

royal pardon...a one-time pardon issued by the British monarch or his representative, also known as an "Act of Grace", that absolved an individual of any punishment due for past piratical actions in exchange for a pledge to renounce piracy forever.

royals of plate...it may well have referred to silver or gold plate of superior quality, or even gold or silver dinnerware belonging to royalty.

S

Senechal...a highly placed servant in charge of domestic affairs within a household, which could include legal powers.

ship's rigging…according to Webster, a system of ropes and pulleys used for hoisting and pulling.

shore leave pay…pay given to a sailor during his officially sanctioned leave to go ashore when his ship was in dock.

sloop…a vessel that has undergone many definitions over the ages depending on its shape, rigging, etc. During the Golden Age, it was the preferred vessel of pirates. It had a shallow draft and was designed to be extremely fast and capable of readily navigating narrow waterways.

Spanish Main…a region of 16th and 17th century Spanish America, primarily Florida, Central America, and the northern coast of South America.

swashbuckler…a term employed by movie script writers and novelists of the late eighteen and nineteen hundreds to describe the pirates of the Golden Age.

titular…a nominal or honorary title with no duties.

W

War of Spanish Succession…the European name for a war between England and Holland versus France (1701-1714) that was initiated when Louis XIV installed his grandson on the Spanish throne.

ENDNOTES

1 Angus Konstam, *The History of Pirates,* (Guilford, Connecticut, The Lyons Press, 2002), p. 9

2 Terrance Zepke, *Pirates of the Carolinas,* (Sarasota, Florida, Pineapple Press, Inc, Second Edition 2005), p. 9

3 Terrance Zepke, p, 144

4 Terrance Zepke, pp. 155-157

5 "Eustace the Monk". Translated from *Li Romans de Witasse le Moine: Roman du treizieme siecle*, ed. D. J. Conlon (Chapel Hill, 1972), translator Leah Shopkow, pp. 1-4

6 *English Historical Review*, "The Battle of Sandwich and Eustace the Monk", vol. 27 (1912), p. 650

7 "Eustace the Monk", Leah Shopkow (translator), p. 2

8 English Historical Review, p. 651

9 "Eustace the Monk", Leah Shopkow (translator), pp. 10-11

10 Leah Shopkow, Section V

11 Leah Shopkow, Section VI

12 See Glossary definition of "seneschel"

13 "Eustace the Monk", Leah Shopkow , Section VI

14 English Historical Review, p. 652

15 Leah Shopkov, Section VII

16 Leah Shopkow, Section VIII

17 English Historical Review, p. 652

18 Leah Shopkow, Section XIX

19 Ibid

20 Leah Shopkow, Section XX

21 English Historical Review, p. 654

22 English Historical Review, p. 654

23 Leah Shopkow, Section XXII

24 Ibid

25 Angus Konstam, p. 64

26 Ibid

27 Ibid

28 Websource: The Pirate's Realm: *Sir Francis Drake*

29 Websource: Ask.com: *Francis Drake*

30 Websource: Pirate Soul: Notable Pirates: *Sir Francis Drake*

31 Websource: Global Travel Source; *Sir Francis Drake*

32 Ibid

33 Websource: Pirate Soul: *Sir Francis Drake*

34 Angus Konstam, p. 64

35 Ibid

36 Websource: Pirate Soul, *Sir Francis Drake*

37 David Cordingly, p. 30

38 David Cordingly, p. 31

39 Ibid

40 Ibid

41 Angus Konstam, p. 45

42 Websource: Chronicles of America: *The Death of Sir Francis Drake*

43 Websource: FRANCO'S CYBERTEMPLE, The life and times of Sir Henry Morgan

44 Ibid

45 Ibid

46 Ibid

47 Angus Konstam, p. 78

48 Websource: FRANCO'S SYBERTEMPLE: *The life and times of Sir Henry Morgan*

49 Angus Konstam, p. 78

50 Ibid

51 Websource: FRANCO'S SYBERSPACE: *The* life and times of *Sir Francis Drake*

52 Angus Konstam, p. 78

53 Angus Konstam, p. 79

54 Ibid

55 Ibid

56 Ibid

57 David Cordingly, p. 48

58 David Cordingly, p.49

59 Websource: Pirates! *The Battle of Maracaibo Bar*

60 Angus Konstam, p. 80

61 Angus Konstam, p. 79

62 Websource: FRANCO'S CYBERTEMPLE: The life and times of Sir Henry Morgan

63 Angus Konstam, p. 81

64 Ibid

65 Websource: FRANCO'S CYBERTEMPLE: The life and times of Sir Henry Morgan

66 Websource: flagsot.net/flags/gb-priv.html: *British Privateers*

67 Miller Pope, *Book of Pirates*, (Winoca Press, 2001), pp. 54-55

68 Ibid

69 Sandra MacLean Clunies and Bruce Roberts, p. 2

70 John Matthews. *Pirates*, (Atheneum Books for Young Readers, New York, New York, 2006)

71 See Chapter 6.

72 Websource: Online Strategy Gaming: Pirate of the Week: *Christopher Moody ? - 1718*

73 Anthony E. Bakker, *Charleston & The Golden Age of Piracy*, (Dave Myers @ Meissner Design, Charleston. SC)

74 Anthony E. Bakker, p. 19

75 Websource: Online Strategy gaming: *Pirate of the Week: Christopher Moody ? - 1718*

76 Websource: Paul Orton, *Thomas Tew the Pirate, of Rhode Island*, (Red Flag links, 1999), Section #11

77 Terrance Zepke, p. 95-96

78 Terrance Zepke, p. 96

79 Websource: Paul Orton, Section #3

80 Websource: Paul Orton, Section #2

81 See Chapter Four

82 Terrance Zepke, p. 96

83 Terrance Zepke, p. 98

84 Ibid

85 Terrance Zepke, p. 98-99

86 Terrance Zepke, p. 99

87 Ibid

88 Paul Orton, Section #10

89 Terrance Zepke, p. 100

90 Websource: Paul Orton, Section VIII

91 Websource: Paul Orton, Section VIII

92 David Cordingly, p.21

93 Ibid

94 Terrance Zepke, pp. 73-74

95 Terrance Zepke, p. 74

96 Ibid

97 Angus Konstam p. 130

98 Terrance Zepke, p. 74

99 Ibid

100 Terrance Zepke, p. 75

101 David Cordingly, p. 22

102 Terrance Zepke, p. 76-77

103 David Cordingly, p. 23

104 Terrance Zepke, p. 77

105 David Cordingly, p. 23

106 Terrance Zepke, p. 78

107 Edgar Allen Poe. The Philadelphia Newspaper, *The Gold-Bug*, June, 1843

108 Terrance Zepke, p. 116

109 Ibid

110 Ibid

111 Ibid

112 Ibid

113 Ibid

114 Terrance Zepke, p. 117

115 Ibid

116 Terrance Zepke, p. 118

117 Angus Konstam, p. 128

118 Terrance Zepke, p, 119

119 Websource: Cambridge Encyclopedia, Vol, #80: State University .com *William Kidd*

120 Terrance Zepke, p, 120

121 Terrance Zepke, p. 123

122 Terrance Zepke, p. 124

123 Terrance Zepke, p. 123

124 Terrance Zepke, p. 128

125 Terrance Zepke, p. 130

126 Terrance Zepke, p. 130-131

127 Terrance Zepke, p. 131

128 Terrance Zepke, p. 132

129 Terrance Zepke, p. 133

130 Susan Taylor Block, *The Legend of Money Island,* (Wrightsville Beach Magazine, March 7, 2007)

131 Terrance Zepke, p. 140

132 Ibid

133 Terrance Zepke, p. 140

134 Terrance Zepke, p. 141

135 Ibid

136 Ibid

137 Ibid

138 Ibid

139 Terrance Zepke, p. 142

140 Ibid

141 Susan Taylor Block, *Money Island*

142 Ibid

143 Ibid

144 Websource: The Pirate's Realm: S*amuel Bellamy.*
Sam Bellamy, Black Sam Belamy

145 Ibid

146 Ibid

147 Websource: The Way of Pirates: Famous Pirate: *Samuel   Bellamy The Romantic Pirate*

148 Sandra MacLean Clunies and Bruce Roberts, p.15

149 Angus Konstam, p. 108

149 Sandra MacLean Clunies and Bruce Roberts, p. 15

150 Sandra MacLean Clunies and Bruce Roberts, p. 16

151 Ibid

152 Ibid

153 Ibid

154 Ibid

155 Ibid

156 Sandra MacLean Clunies and Bruce Roberts, p. 17

157 Sandra MacLean Clunies and Bruce Roberts, pp, 16-17

158 Sandra MacLean Clunies and Bruce Roberts, p. 17

159 Ibid

160 Sandra McLean Clunies and Bruce Roberts, p. 14

161 Terrance Zepke, pp. 107-108

162 Terrance Zepke, p. 109

163 Anthony E. Bakker, p. 13

164 Sandra MacLean Clunies and Bruce Roberts, p. 14

165 Ibid

166 Terrance Zepke, p. 111

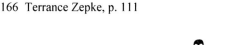

167 Terrance Zepke, p. 112

168 Ibid

169 Sandra MacLean Clunies and Bruce Roberts, p. 14

170 Websource: ExecutedToday.com: 1720 Captain John "Calico Jack" Rackham

171 The Way of the Pirates: Famous Pirate: Benjamin Hornigold. *Blackbeard's tutor*

172 Websource: Age of Pirates: *Pirate Encylopedia: Benjamin Hornigold*

173 Ibid

174 Terrance Zepke, p. 18

175 Websource: AbsoluteAstronomy: Nassau, Bahamas

176 Websource: Colin Woodward, *The Republic of Pirates*

177 Sanda MacLean Clunies and Bruce Roberts, p.13

178 Websource: Brethren of the Coast: Benjamin Hornigold

179 Ibid

180 Websource: Famtic.com *Benjamin Hornigold*

181 Sandra MaClean Clunies and Bruce Roberts, p.8

182 Terrance Zepke, p, 18

183 Terrance Zepke, p. 19

184 Ibid

185 Sandra MacLean Clunies and Bruce Roberts, p. 8

186 Terrance Zepke, pp. 25-26

187 Terrance Zepke, pp. 21-23

188 Terrance Zepke, pp. 26

189 Terrance Zepke, p. 24

190 Terrance Zepke, pp. 22

191 Terrance Zepke, p. 24

192 Terrance Zepke, p. 25

193 Terrance Zepke, p. 27

194 Ibid

195 Terrance Zepke, p. 28-29

196 Terrance Zepke, p. 30

197 Sandra MacLean Clunies and Bruce Roberts, p. 9

198 Terrance Zepke, p. 33

199 Ibid

200 Terrance Zepke, p. 35

201 Sandra MacLean Clunies and Bruce Roberts, p. 9

202 Sandra MacLean Clunies and Bruce Roberts, p. 4

203 Ibid

204 Terrance Zepke, pp. 87-88

205 Sandra MacLean Clunies and Bruce Roberts, p. 4

206 Terrance Zepke, p. 88

207 Sandra MacLean Clunies and Bruce Roberts, p. 4

208 Websource: Squidoo: Pirates Worthy of Note: *Stede Bonnet*

209   See Chapter Four

210 Terrance Zepke, pp. 88-89

211 Terrance Zepke, p. 89

212 Sandra MacLean Clunies and Bruce Roberts, p. 4

213 Terrance Zepke, p, 90

214 Angus Konstam, p. 113

215 Ibid

216 NC Maritime Museum in Southport [S.C. Hughes, *Carolina Pirates and Colonial Commerce (1670 – 1740)]*

217 Terrance Zepke, p. 91

218 Sandra MacLean Clunies and Bruce Roberts, p. 6

219 Ibid

221 Anthony E. Bakker, p. 19 221 Anthony E. Bakker, p.22

222 Websource: Wanted for Piracy: *Edward Low (Lowe, Loe) AKA: Ned Low*

223 Websource: The Pirate's Realm: *Edward Low, Pirate Ed Low, Ned Low*

224 Websource: Pirate Soul: Notable Pirates: *Edward Low*

225 Websource: Squidoo: *Edward Low* at a Glance

226 Ibid

227 Ibid

228 Websource: Online Gaming Strategy: *Edward Low*

229 Ibid

230 Websource: Pirate Soul: Notable Pirates: *Edward Low*

231 Websource: The Pirate's Realm: Notable Pirates: *Edward Low*

232 Ibid

233 Websource: Online Strategy Gaming: *Edward Low*

234 Anthony E. Bakker, p. 22

235 Websource: The Pirate's Realm: Notable Pirates: *Edward Low*

236 Angus Konstam, p. 106

237 Websource: geocities.com: *Captain Bartholomew Roberts*

238 Angus Konstam, p. 115

239 Captain John Roberts, p.58

240 Websource: geocities.com: *Captain Bartholomew Roberts*

241 See Chapter Four.

242 Sandra MacLean Clunies and Bruce Roberts, p. 21 (Inside back cover.)

243 Websource: geocities.com: *Captain Bartholomew Roberts*

244 Ibid

245 Ibid

246 Websource: The Pirate's Realm: *Calico Jack Rackham Pirate*

247 Websource: Site 101.com: *Pirate Captain John Rackham*

248 Angus Konstam, p. 104

249 Terrance Zepke, p. 54

250 Ibid

251 Terrance Zepke, pp. 54-55

252 Sandra MacLean Clunies and Bruce Roberts, p. 19

253 Terrance Zepke, p. 56

254 Ibid

255 Websource: The Pirate's Realm: *Christopher Condent, Pirate Christopher Condent*

256 Ibid

257 Ibid

258 Ibid

259 Ibid

260 Websource: cosmosmith.com: *Christopher Condent*

261 Angus Konstam, p. 132

262 Ibid

263 Ibid

264 Ibid

265 Terrance Zepke, p. 56

266 Ibid

267 Websource: the Way of Pirates, Famous Pirate: Edward England

268 Websource: vieonica.com: *Captain Edward England*

269 Angus Konstam, p. 133

270 Ibid

271 Ibid

272 Ibid

273 Terrance Zepke, p. 67

274 Terrance Zepke, p. 68

275 Ibid

276 Ibid

277 Ibid

278 Terrance Zepke, p. 69

279 Terrance Zepke, p. 69

280 Terrance Zepke, p. 70

281 Websource: Ask Jeeves: The Pirate's Hold, David Stapleton, *William Fly*

282 Terrance Zepke, p. 85

283 Terrance Zepke, pp. 81-82

284 Terrance Zepke, p. 82

285 Websource: Wanted for Piracy: Career Pirate from Nassau, *William Lewis*

286 Terrance Zepke, p. 84

287 Ibid

288 Websource: Wanted for Piracy: Career Pirate from Nassau: *William Lewis*

289 Terrance Zepke, p. 85

290 Ibid

291 Websource: Department of the Navy, Naval Histoical Center: *John Paul Jones*

292 Websource: Asked Questions: 250th Anniversary of the Birth of *John Paul Jones*

293 Ibid

294 Websource: Department of the Navy, Naval Historical Center: *John Paul Jones*

295 Websource: Department of the Navy, Naval Historical Center: 250th Anniversary of the Birth of John Paul Jones

296 Websource: Department of the Navy, Naval Historical Center: Biographies in Naval History, (unpublished) *Ca[tain John Paul Jones*

297 Ibid

298 Websource: U.S. Department of State: Diplomacy in Action, French Alliance, French Assistance, and European diplomacy during the American Revolution, 1778-1782

299 Websource: Department of the Navy, Naval Historical Center: Biographies in Naval History, (unpublished) *John Paul Jones*

300 Angus Konstam, pp. 150-151

301 Websource: AbsoluteAstronomy.com: *John Paul Jones*

302 Websource: Alan Axelrod, *The Complete Idiot's Guide to the American Revolution*, p. 27

303 Websource: USS Bonhomme Richard: History, The Frigate Bonhomme Richard

304 Ibid

305 Ibid

306 Ibid

307 Websource: Department of the Navy, Naval Historical Center: Biographies in Naval History, (unpublished) *John Paul Jones*

308 Angus Konstam, p. 151

309 Ibid

309 Websource: The Two Burials of John Paul Jones

310 Ibid

311 Ibid

312 Ibid

313 Websource: SeacoastNH.com: Farewell *Paul Jones*: A President Says Goodbye to his Hero in 1906

314 Ibid

315 Websource: truTVCRIMELIBRARY: Criminal Minds and Methods: *Jean LaFitte,* Gentleman Pirate of New Orleans

316 Angus Konstam, p. 156

317 Ibid

318 Websource: truTVCRIMELIBRARY: Criminal Minds and Methods: *Jean LaFitte*, the Gentleman Pirate of New Orleans

319 Angus Konstam, p. 156

320 Ibid

321 Ibid

322 Ibid

323 Websource: truTVCRIMELIBRARY: Criminal Minds and Methods: *Jean LaFitte*, the Gentleman Pirate of New Orleans, Barataria

324 Angus Konstam, , p. 156-157

325 Websource: truTVCRIMELIBRARY: Criminal Minds and Methods: *Jean LaFitte*, the Gentleman Pirate of New Orleans, The Battle of New Orleans

326 Angus Konstam, p. 157

327 Ibid

328 Websource: The Handbook of Texan Online: The LaFitte Brothers

331 Websource: Beagle Bay. A List of Women Pirates – Real and Legendary

332 Websource: Cindy Vallar. Pirates & Privateers. The History of Maritime Piracy – *I viking*

333 Katy Berry. Historical Female Pirates: Alvilda

334 Ibid

335 Ibid

336 Ibid

337 Ibid

338 Ibid

339 Ibid

340 Ibid

341 Websource: Salem Street Gazette, Susan Ulbrich: A Pirate and A[n] Aristocrat

342 Ibid

343 Ibid

344 Ibid

345 Ibid

346 Websource: Fionaurora.com: *Lady Mary Killigrew* of Cornwall

347 Ibid

348 Ibid

349 Ibid

350 Websource: nauticalinstitute.ca: Cathy Converse, The Lady Was A Pirate, p. 2

351 Websource: essortment.com: *Grace O'Malley*, Irish pirate, p.1

352 Ibid

353 Ibid

354 Websource: essortment.com: p. 2

355 Websource: The Renaissance Record. Rosemarie Colombraro, Grace O'Malley, p. 1

356 Ibid

357 Ibid

358 Websource: Judy Staley, Notable Women Ancestors, *Grace O'Malley*

359 Ibid

360 Ibid

361 Websource: nauticalinstitute.ca: Cathy Converse, The Lady Was A Pirate, p, 3

362 Ibid

363   Websource: Google, eSSORTMENT, *Grace O'Malley,* Irish Pirate

364 Ibid

365 Ibid

366 Websource: nauticalinstitute.ca: Cathy Converse, The Lady Was A Pirate

367 Terrance Zepke, pp. 45-46

368 Sandra MacLean Clunies and Bruce Roberts, p. 18

369 Terrance Zepke, p. 47

370 Ibid

371 Ibid

372 Sandra MacLean Clunies and Bruce Roberts, p. 18

373 Terrance Zepke, p. 47

374 Angus Konstam, p. 104

375 Terrance Zepke, p. 49

376 Terrance Zepke, pp. 54-55

377 Sandra MacLean Clunies and Bruce Roberts, p. 19

378 Ibid

379 Terrance Zepke, p. 57

380 Terrance Zepke, pp. 59-60

381 Ibid

382 Sandra MacLean Clunies and Bruce Roberts, p. 18

383 Terrance Zepke, p. 60

384 Terrance Zepke, pp. 60-61

385 Terrance Zepke, p. 61

386 Trttance Zepke, p. 62

387 Websource: Rob Ossian's Pirate's Cove: *Mary Read, Female Pirate*

388 Sandra MacLean Clunies and Bruce Roberts, p. 19

389 Angus Konstam, p. 174

390 Ibid

391 Websource: MaritimeDigital Archive Encyclopedia: *Ching Shih (Cheng I Sao)*

392 Angus Konstam, p. 174

393 Websource: MaritimeDigital Archive Encyclopedia: *Ching Shih*

394 Angus Konstam, p. 175

395 Ibid

396 Websource: nauticalinstitute.ca: Cathy Converse, "The Lady Was A Pirate", *Cheng I Sao*

397 Ibid

398 Ibid

399 Angus Konstam, p, 175

400 Websource: Rob Ossian's Pirate's Cove: *Cheng I sao*

401 Websource: nautical institute.ca: Cathy Converse, "The Lady Was A Pirate", *Cheng I Sao*

402 Websource: Caitlin, Rachel Wall, p. 1

403 Websource: Cindy Vallar: Pirates and Privateers: The History of Maritime Piracy, *Rachel Wall*

404 Websource: Catlin, Rachel Wall, p. 1

405 Ibid

406 Ibid

407 Websource: Online Strategy Gaming: Pirate of the Week: *Rachel Wall*

408 Ibid

409 Websource: Rob Ossian's Pirate Cove, *Rachel Wall*, Female Pirate

410 Ibid

411 Websource: Suite101.com: *Rachel Wall*, Notorious Woman Pirate

412 Websource: community.livejournal.com: Steampunk fashion: *Sadie Farrell*

413 Websource: griped4kids.org: Gang History

414 Websource: Amazon.com: NewYorkology: A New York Travel Guide: Sara Lorimer, *Booty, Girl Pirates on the High Seas*

415 Herbert Asbury, *Gangs of New York: An Informal History of the Underworld (Thunder's Mouth Press, October 10, 2001 edition)*

416 Websorce: shell.linux.se/treggy88/Leo/gony/femalegangsters/html: Maggie Estep, Gangs of New York's Female Gangsters

417 Websource: community.livejournal.com Steampunk fashon: *Sadie Farrell*

418 Ibid

419 Ibid

420 Ibid

421 Ibid

422 Websource: PIRATE SISTAHS Tribe.Net: *Sadie the Goat*

423 Ibid

424 Websource: nauticalinstitute,ca: Cathy Converse, "The Lady Was A Pirate"

425 Websource: canadiancountrywoman.com: Carolyn McTaggart, *Gunpowder Gertie, Pirate Queen of the Kootenays*

426 Ibid

427 Ibid

428 Ibid

429 Ibid

430 Ibid

431 Ibid

432 Websource: Privateer Dragon's Island: Private Mythtory: *Gertrude Stubbgs --- Gunpowder Gertie*

433 Websource: livius.org/cg-cm/cilicia/Cilician_pirates,html, Jona Lendering, "Cilician Pirates", an article appearing "in Ancient Warfare Magazine"

434 Ibid

435 Websource: livius.org/caa-caesar/caesar-t01.htm: Caesar and the pirates, a translation of Plutarch of Chaeronea by Robin Seager appearing in "Ancient Warfare Magazine"

436 Ibid

437 Angus Konstam. p. 28

438 Angus Konstam, p. 27

439 Websource: livius.org?cg-cm/cilicia/cilician_pirates,htlm: Cilician Pirates

440 Angus Konstam, p. 28

441 Ibid

442 Websource: MilitaryHistoryOnline. Pompey and Ancient Piracy

443 Angus Konstam, p.29

444 Angus Konstam, p.118

445 Websource: Long John Silver Trust. *Woodes Rogers*, (1679-1732) Privateer and Governor

446 Websource: earthlink.net: *Woodes Rogers*

447 Angus Konstam, p. 118

448 Websource: earthlink.net: *Woodes Rogers*

449 Ibid

450 Ibid

451 Angus Konstam, p. 118

452 Websource: earthlink.net: *Woodes Rogers*

453 Ibid

454 Ibid

455 Ibid

456 Angus Konstam, pp. 118-119

457 Angus Konstam, p. 119

458 Websource: earthlink.net: *Woodes Rogers*

459 Websource: The Thomas Jefferson Papers. Gerald W. Gawalt, "America and the Barbary Pirates: An International Battle Against an Unconventional Foe"

460 Ibid

461 Ibid

462 Ibid

463 Ibid

464 Ibid

465 Ibid

466 Ibid

467 Websource: parpro.zweb.com/Decatur.html: *Stephen Decatur* by William Wills

468 Websource: AbsoluteAstronomy.com: *Stephen Decatur*, Second Barbary War

469 Ibid

470 Ibid

471 Ibid

472 Ibid

About The Author

𝓜ike Hogan was born and raised in Indianapolis, Indiana. He attended Kenyon College and DePauw University before going to graduate school at the University of North Carolina in Chapel Hill. There he earned masters degrees in Mathematical Statistics and Public Health, as well as a Ph.D. in Biostatistics. Mike then worked for over thirty years for the National Institute of Environmental Health Sciences, ending his career as the Associate Director for Planning and Policy within the Division of Intramural Research.

Since retiring, Mike and his wife, Gayle, have relocated to Southport, NC, at the mouth of the Cape Fear River. They are fortunate to be near both of their married daughters, their four grandchildren, and the ocean. As has always been the case, their two soft-coated Wheaten terriers are in complete charge of their household.

Currently Mike teaches remedial math at a local community college and writes historical articles for the regional magazine *Southcoast*. Needless to say, the latter endeavor has given rise to his complete fascination with pirates, particularly those of the Golden Age.

Photo by Terry Beers

LaVergne, TN USA
15 November 2009
164153LV00005B/1/P